# THREE
# FACES OF GOD

# THREE
# FACES OF GOD

Traces of the Trinity in Literature
and Life

## DAVID L. MILLER

Fortress Press                    Philadelphia

Library of Congress Cataloging-in-Publication Data

Miller, David LeRoy.
  Three faces of God.

  Includes index.
  1. Trinity — History of doctrines.  2. Trinity in
literature.  I. Title.
  BT109.M515 1986      231'.044      85-45493
  ISBN 0-8006-1895-5

1828185    Printed in the United States of America    1-1895

for
Patricia

# CONTENTS

## Part Three
## Loving by Triangulation

# ACKNOWLEDGMENTS

A portion of this book, in an earlier version, was originally a lecture given at the Eranos Conference in 1980, and is published in the *Eranos Jahrbuch* 49–1980 (Frankfurt am Main: Insel Verlag, 1981), pp. 81–148. It is used here by permission of the Eranos Foundation, Ascona, Switzerland.

Also, parts of the Introduction were published previously in "Theology's Ego/Religion's Soul," *Spring 1980* (Dallas, TX 75201), pp. 78–89. The material is used by permission of James Hillman, editor.

The illustrations on pages 18–20 are taken from W. L. Dulière, *De la dyade à l'unité par la triade* (Paris: Adrien Maisonneuve, 1965), pp. 38, 152, 193, 198, and 213. They are reproduced here by permission of the Librairie d'Amérique et d'Orient (Adrien Maisonneuve), 11 rue Saint-Suplice, 75006 Paris.

The lines from "The Tenth Elegy" from *Duino Elegies* by Rainer Maria Rilke, tranlated by J. B. Leishman and Stephen Spender, are reprinted by permission of W. W. Norton & Company, Inc. Copyright 1939 by W. W. Norton Company, Inc. Copyright renewed 1967 by Stephen Spender and J. B. Leishman.

"The Happy Three," copyright © 1962 by Beatrice Roethke, Administratrix of the Estate of Theodore Roethke from the book *The Collected Poetry of Theodore Roethke* by Theodore Roethke. Reprinted by permission of Doubleday & Company, Inc.

Excerpts from "Burnt Norton" in *Four Quartets* by T. S. Eliot, copyright 1943 by T. S. Eliot; renewed 1971 by Esme Valerie Eliot. Reprinted by permission of Harcourt Brace Jovanovich, Inc.

Excerpts from "The Waste Land" in *Collected Poems* 1909–1962 by T. S. Eliot, copyright 1936 by Harcourt Brace Jovanovich, Inc.; copyright © 1963, 1964 by T. S. Eliot. Reprinted by permission of the publisher.

Excerpts from James Thurber, "*What* Cocktail Party?" Copr. © 1953 James Thurber. Copr. © 1981 Helen Thurber and Rosemary A. Thurber. From *Thurber Country*, published by Simon & Schuster.

Robert Creeley, "The Three Ladies" from *For Love: Poems 1950–1960*. Copyright © 1962 Robert Creeley. Reprinted with the permission of Charles Scribner's Sons.

Excerpt from *Dreamtigers* by Jorge Luis Borges, translated by Mildred Boyer and Harold Morland. Copyright © 1964. Reprinted by permission of University of Texas Press.

Excerpts from *The Book of Questions*. Copyright © 1963 by Editions Gallimard. Translation copyright © 1972, 1973, 1974, 1976 by Rosemarie Waldrop. Reprinted from *The Book of Questions: Volume I* by permission of Wesleyan University Press.

Excerpts from "Self-Portrait in a Convex Mirror" by John Ashbery. Copyright © 1972, 1973, 1974, 1975 by John Ashbery. Reprinted by permissions of Viking Penguin Inc.

Excerpts from Rainer Maria Rilke, *Poems from the Book of Hours*. Copyright 1941 by New Directions Publishing Corporation. Translated by Babette Deutsch. Reprinted by permission of New Directions Publishing Corporation.

Lines from "The Owl in the Sarcophagus," "Nomad Exquisite," and "Thirteen Ways of Looking at a Blackbird" from Wallace Stevens, *The Collected Poems of Wallace Stevens*. Copyright 1923, 1931, 1935, 1936, 1937, 1942, 1943, 1944, 1945, 1946, 1947, 1948, 1949, 1950, 1951, 1952, 1954, by Wallace Stevens. Reprinted by permission of the publisher, Alfred A. Knopf, Inc.

Selections from Harold Pinter, *The Complete Works: Two* © 1977 by H. Pinter Ltd. are used by permission of Grove Press.

Selections from Harold Pinter, *The Complete Works: Four* © 1976 by H. Pinter Ltd. are used by permission of Grove press.

Excerpts from *An Anthology of German Poetry from Hölderlin to Rilke*, Angel Flores, ed. Copyright © by Angel Flores. Published by Doubleday.

Excerpts from James Joyce, *Ulysses*. Copyright 1914, 1918 by Margaret Caroline Anderson. Copyright, 1934 by The Modern Library, Inc. Copyright 1942, 1946 by Norah Joseph Joyce. Reprinted by permission of the publisher, Random House, Inc.

Excerpts from Robert Pirsig, *Zen and the Art of Motorcycle Maintenance*. Copyright © 1974 by Robert M. Pirsig. Used with permission of William Morrow & Company, Inc.

Finally, the author is especially grateful to the artist, Ms. Dianna Miller, who created line drawings from the illustrations for purposes of printing and publication.

Introduction

# THEOLOGY
# AS REMEMBERING,
# CONTEMPLATING, AND LOVING

Even St. Augustine despaired of understanding the notion of the
Trinity. In *The Confessions,* he wrote:

> Who can understand the omnipotent Trinity? And yet who does not
> speak about it, if indeed it is of it that he speaks? Rare is the soul who,
> when he speaks of it, also knows of what he speaks.[1]

Indeed, how could one know of what she or he speaks? How is it possible to understand a oneness that is three? or a threeness that is, at
bottom, one? Even more problematic, how might a person believe in
a God who insists on being imagined monotheistically (as one), but
who persists in manifesting himself in history polytheistically (as
three)?

In spite of these difficulties, even logical impossibilities, the Trinity
is alive and well, although not in places one might have expected.
The notion flourishes in a mythology recovered from an ancient
pagan past and in a secular literature of our own most recent times.
Yet, in both popular piety and academic theology, where one might
have thought to find trinitarian talk, it flags and is sometimes
neglected altogether. To be sure, such tendency to slight the Trinity
*in religion* is, from Christian perspective, suspect. So it is ironic to discover that an antidote to religion's forgetfulness comes from the sides
of pagan antiquity and latter-day secular literature. These resources,
as we shall see throughout the pages of this book, support a trinitarian view of the world and its life.

Potentially, then, myth and literature can make possible a re-
visioning of a trinitarian theology in our time, even though this old

1

notion concerning ultimate religious reality (Trinity) is so often per-
plexing to the very theology and belief which are sources for the idea
in the first place — as Augustine's saying tells. The irony is that such
a re-visioning requires religion to relearn its own sacred truths from
secular culture.

Besides attending to the fact that religion may be learned from culture, however, this book also attends to the perhaps equally curious
notion that theology is learned on oneself, and possibly *only* on oneself, if it be learned at all. This, of course, deserves some explanation.

On the one hand, theology has typically represented religious matters as referring to doctrines, dogmas, or tenets of belief. This leads
one to imagine that the stories and images of religion have to do with
ideas and thoughts. Faith, then, becomes a matter of assent. Mysteries of religion are located in the mind and spirit. They are seen as
"wholly other," belonging to a domain that philosophy has called the
realm of *intelligibles*.

On the other hand, and often in contrast to this first perspective,
another sort of theology has represented religious matters as corresponding to feeling, mystified experience, the occult, a strange
warmth in the heart, love, I and Thou. This attitude leads one to
imagine that the stories and images of religion have to do with the
pietisms of everyday personal life and morality. Faithfulness becomes
a matter of literalistic *imitatio Christi*. Mysteries belong to will and
sense. Religion exists in a world that philosophy has called the realm
of *sensibles*.[2]

As theology has swayed, like a drunken sailor, back and forth
between these doctrinal and pietistic approaches, the effect on the
religious imagination has been to split mind from heart, spirit from
flesh, ideal from real, thought from feeling, infinite from finite,
supernatural from natural, transcendental from immanent. That is,
when religious images are interpreted in one of these ways *or* the
other, one finds oneself thinking and feeling that various poles of life-
experience are split, that they are "infinitely qualitatively distinct," as
Søren Kierkegaard said. Religion is thus separated from life and dies.

But there is another effect, also. Theology, when viewed in such
ways, is a matter of the ego and is dominated by the ego's perspectives, even though it proclaims a religion whose gospel concerns the
soul and its depths. In a doctrinal theology that places religion's

images in the realm of intelligibles, religious meaning comes under the control of the human mind. At least that is the attempt. It is, according to Anselm, a matter of *fides quaerens intellectus* (faith seeking to be intellect). In a pietistic theology, religion's meaning is taken personally. One says, "Jesus Christ is *my personal* Lord and Savior."

Both doctrinal and pietistic theologizing tend to deny or defend against the depth of religious meaning, its fundamental mystery and ambiguity, its terror and grace, its autonomous nature that comes and goes as it will, like the Holy Ghost wandering over the face of the deep. Ego theology is a defense mechanism which banalizes religion.

C. G. Jung was aware of this situation and commented on it in relation to a theologian he had in analysis. This man had had a dream in which there was an image similar to that in the biblical story of the Holy Ghost rippling the waters of the pool at Bethesda. The patient was totally resistant to associating his dream with the religious image. Jung commented: "I am of course aware that theologians are in a more difficult situation than others. On the one hand they are closer to religion; but on the other hand, they are more bound by church and dogma [*i.e.*, by doctrinal and pietistic ways of sensing religion's content]. The risk of inner experience . . . the possibility that such experience might have psychic reality is anathema to them. . . . Face to face with this question, the patient will often show an unsuspected but profound contempt for the psyche."[3] Ego theology stands in contempt of the soul.

There must be another way, a theological way more appropriate to the soul-matter of religions, some "third" strategy different from the doctrinal and pietistic perspectives that split religion from its soul in the interest of ego, as if saying, where religious image is, there let ego be: theology's versions of making the unconscious conscious. This book is concerned for mind *and* heart, for understanding *and* life-experience, both at once. So it seeks a "third" way, a trinitarian way of thinking and feeling, not to mention speaking, about the Trinity. The experience of contemporary depth psychology holds a clue as to method in the trinitarian theology that we seek, and a clue, too, for understanding this strange idea that one can learn theology on oneself.

In Vienna, during the winter semester of 1915, Sigmund Freud addressed a group of medical students on the subject of psychoanalysis. He called attention to difficulties in learning this new science of the soul. The students were told that they would not be able to understand this subject matter by deductive thinking, the sort of reasoning they had found useful in studying neurology, for example. Neither would empirical observation work, as it had in the study of anatomy. A third way would be required. "One learns psychoanalysis," Freud told them, "on oneself." Then he added, "This is not quite the same thing as what is called self-observation,"[4] as if he were saying that soul-work is not a matter of ego looking at ego but that there is a deeper seeing and sensing, a way that does not sever intellect and personal experience.

To Freud, the perspective of depth comes from those aspects of life that are sensed as autonomous in relation to the ego and its controls: emotions and moods, slips of the tongue and physical sickness, neurotic behavior and psychopathic states, entangled relationships and vocational messes, fantasies and dreams. By entering these life-experiences thoroughly, Freud's patients and students discovered not only themselves (ego-states) but also Oedipus, Eros, Thanatos, and others of those transpersonal configurations that we have come to know by the names of the gods.

By way of archetypal understanding, Jung made deeper what was already implied in Freud's work: that one learns soul-science only on oneself. In activating images of self archetypally one learns also about the gods, discovering religion's traditional images ensouled, touching that which is "other" in that which one is. Ancient theologians had witnessed to this long before Freud or Jung. Clement of Alexandria was typical of others when he wrote, "It is then, as appears, the greatest of all lessons to know oneself, for if one knows oneself, he will know God."[5] There is something astonishing implied in this: like the soul-science of Freud and Jung, *one also can learn theology, if at all deeply, only on oneself.*

It goes without saying that such learning would be different in kind from studies of traditional doctrine and belief, with their supernaturalistic perspectives concerning religious meaning. But such a way would be different, too, from the approach of various pietisms, since it is not a matter of linking religious content to the *ego's* biography or to *personal* experience. Rather, it is a likening of the images of religion to the autonomous pathologies of soul over which the ego has little will-control and about which the ego can make very little sense. Perhaps such a theological perspective could be thought of as Depth Theology.[6] It could be seen as an attempt to be responsive to Jung when he said, "We must gratefully acknowledge the invaluable support psychology has received from students of . . . religion, even if they on their part have not yet learnt how to make use of its insights."[7]

Jung makes certain of these insights explicit for a depth theology. "When we speak of religious contents," he notes, "we move in a world of images . . . that relate to a few basic [psychological] principles or archetypes."[8] At another point he observes, "Everything conscious is an image, and that image is psyche."[9]

Together these attitudes suggest, not that one could use images from religion to understand a self taken to be different from those materials, but rather that the images of religion *are* soul.[10] That is, religious images have as one of their proper locations, as one of their appropriate referents, the transpersonal fantasies that an ego suffers in its emotions and moods, in slips and illnesses, in compulsions and crazinesses, in messy relationships and in dreams. Religion's images and stories are depth psychology misread as doctrinal or pietistic theology.[11]

Thus, a third way in theology would look for images in the ideas of doctrine and in the experiences of piety and morality. One function of such an approach to religious meaning would be to bring the realms of intelligibles and sensibles into a total complex of experience. When an abstract idea, such as the doctrine of the Trinity, is located in some concrete image-sense, this image-sense gives feeling to the idea. Heart is not split from mind when one senses imaginally. Similarly, when so-called religious experience is given image, when its fantasy is mused upon, the ego-life having that experience achieves transpersonal ideation. Spirit is not severed from body. The work, then, is to "lead back" ideas and experiences to fundamental images.[12] A depth theology is an imaginal theology.

That an imaginal theology is also trinitarian and archetypal (in Augustine's sense, from which Jung acknowledges that he took his own idea)[13] may be seen by describing in more concrete detail three facets of the work of leading back. These facets correspond, as St. Augustine noted, to the Holy Trinity discovered in the soul's experience of itself. The three are *remembering, contemplating,* and *loving.*[14]

The first aspect of the task is to *remember* the ideas of theology as if they were archetypal complexes of the soul (see part 1). If one is to learn theology on oneself, one expects to discover religion's images to be precise metaphoric expressions of that which one thinks and feels: thrown into a world where things need naming; expulsed from Edenic sense; towering Babel; flooding in life; bondage; walking dry through the midst of seas; wandering in wildernesses; drawn to gold idols; wanting a king like the others; exiled; on an ash heap; whirlwind; something sacred getting born out of a virginal place in the self; nailed; betrayed; miraculously going on; waiting for the spirit to come; apocalypse now; my God, why hast thou forsaken me. Every image and story of religion, every doctrinal and creedal idea, becomes stunningly connected with the soul's sense of things when one looks and listens with the eyes and ears of a depth theology.

Of course there will always be those who think of such an approach to religion as psychologizing, subjective, solipsistic, or gnostic. But this would be to continue to imagine that such senses of self — moods, dreams, illnesses — are under the will's control or are susceptible to an analysis or explanation by the ego's intellect and reason. If one were to note, as did Freud and Jung, that it is precisely at these moments that the ego is *un*conscious, then this approach would seem not a psychologizing of religion but a theologizing of the self, an amplification rather than a reduction, mythos rather than logos, story and poetry rather than logic.

Further, religion's imagery would take on an immediacy, not now mediated by way of theology's doctrines or by some religious experience that one feels obliged to have. The relevance of religious meaning is located thereby not in the historical past nor in the eschatological future, but here and now; not in the ego, but just where the ego is wounded, where its perspectives are deepened soulwise. Religion's images give meaningful expression to personal sufferings, deepening life's sense.[15] But this remembrance of the imaginal intimacy is only the beginning of the work.

*Contemplation* is a second moment in a depth theology (see part

2). If the first moment is a leading back into the images of the ideas and experiences, the second is a "leading down" into those images' complexities. One begins to discover a multitude of mythic backgrounds in the variety of theological fantasia. Here the imaginal theology becomes archetypal.

Jung began this work for the contemporary theologian. For example, he took his reader behind the Christ-image of soul to gnostic fantasies of an antichrist; behind the Mass to fantasies of the alchemist, Zosimos, eating himself; behind the sufferings of Job into alchemical metaphors of dichotomy in God. Nor was this archetypal contemplation unselfconscious in Jung. In a letter to Freud, dated February 11, 1910, he wrote:

> I think we must give it [psychoanalysis] time to infiltrate into people from many centers, to revivify among intellectuals a feeling for symbol and myth, ever so gently to transform Christ back into the soothsaying god of the vine, which he was, and in this way absorb those ecstatic instinctual forces of Christianity for the one purpose of making the cult and the myth what they once were—a drunken feast of joy where man regained the ethos and holiness of an animal. That was the beauty and purpose of classical religion, which from God knows what temporary biological needs has turned into a Misery Institute. Yet what infinite rapture and wantonness lies dormant in our religion, waiting to be led back to their true destination! A genuine and proper . . . development . . . must . . . bring to fruition . . . the agony and ecstasy over the dying and resurgent god, the mythic power of the wine, the awesome anthropophagy of the Last Supper—only this . . . development can serve the vital forces of religion.[16]

This is not entirely new advice. Though current theologizing has in general not contemplated religious images in their archetypal, mythic complexity, the early church fathers regularly drew upon the tales of the Greeks in sermons to give an individuated immediacy to religion's images. Justin Martyr, for example, likened the doctrine of Christ the Great Teacher to Mercury, Aesculapius, Hercules, Bacchus, Ariadne, Perseus, and Bellerophon, to name only a few.[17] One can imagine an archetypal contemplation of Christ the Shepherd by way of Pan, Apollo, Orpheus, Polyphemus, Paris, and Merlin.

Since the nineteenth century theology has recognized that the thought forms of traditional Christian ideas have been borrowed from Greek philosophical modes of seeing. Similarly, in classical

studies it was assumed that philosophical forms of thinking, in their
turn, were taken from the myths of the Greek gods and goddesses. In
his work *The Metaphysics*, Aristotle admitted that everything in his
philosophy could have been found in Homer. What in myth had been
plot, in philosophy became logic. What had been image or character
became idea.[18] So, if behind the theology is philosophy and if behind
philosophy is myth, then theology must unwittingly be carrying
mythic images in its ideas.

Contemplating the archetypal, mythical complexities in the
images of theological ideas is a therapy for traditional theology
because it entails making conscious the deep liveliness in ideas that
may have appeared lifeless.

But therapy—whether that of an individual or of ideas in
theology—is composed of more than remembering and contemplating. Augustine named this additional factor "amor"; Jung called it
"eros." Both were speaking of a third moment in archetypal theology:
*loving* (see part 3).

The function of eros, as Jung often noted, is to connect. It is the
experience in which one senses a relation or notes an intimacy
between two aspects of life now experienced as a total complex. It
does not suffice to be led back and led down into archetypal images
and mythic resources if love is lacking. Without love there is no link
to life. But in love, with its impulse and passion to think and feel connections, the soul discovers its body. Psyche finds amor at last.

The church fathers had a phrase for describing this work of loving
the images, of sticking with them, of fidelity and faithfulness through
images of religion, of giving body to the soul of ideas. They called it
turning image to likeness, or seeing the likeness in images.[19] Origen
wrote:

> "And God said, Let us make man in our own image and likeness." Then
> he [Moses] adds afterwards, "And God made man; in the image of God
> made he him. . . . " Now the fact that he said, "He made him in the
> image of God," and was silent about the likeness, points to nothing else
> but this, that man received the honor of God's image in his first crea-
> tion, whereas the perfection of God's likeness was reserved for him.[20]

We are given soul's images to remember and contemplate. Our task
is to note the likenesses, the connections. The work is not complete
until religion's images are led through into life.

Such connecting is the function of metaphor in relation to image, and the paradigm of such work is that of the poet. As Rainer Maria Rilke said, there is in poetic metaphor the "waking of a likeness within us" ("erweckten sie uns . . . ein Gleichnis").[21] A flower and a woman are experienced in erotic connection when Robert Burns writes, "My love is like a red, red rose." Seeing poetically is, as Wallace Stevens witnessed:

> a likeness of the earth,
> That by resemblance twanged him through and through,
> Releasing an abysmal melody,
> A meeting, an emerging in the light,
> A dazzle of remembrance and of sight.[22]

So it is that the religious tradition has spoken in parable, allegory, analogy (*analogia entis*), similitude, correspondence, and symbol. Archetypal theology is also poetic theology.[23]

The eros of the poetizing perspective is sensed as one attends to the soul's likeness of images. It is a constant trust of and fidelity to the "little people" and "voices" of fantasy, an embrace of the dreams where the ego and its perspectives suffer, an acceptance of and a working with the activating imaginal moods and messes which are ever present, a loving living of the images of an ever-deeper self. As Rilke expressed this:

> Look! They'd be pointing, perhaps to the catkins hanging,
> From empty hazels, or else they'd be meaning the rain
> That falls on the dark earth in early Spring.
> And we, who have always thought
> Of happiness climbing, would feel
> The emotion that almost startles
> When happiness falls.[24]

Feeling the emotion that almost startles when happiness falls back, down, and through the self — as if meaning were from below as from above — may be the beginning of loving.

Theology's ideas are indeed full of mythic and imaginal scope, psychic depth, and poetic sensibility. But they are often lost, in our belief as much as in our unbelief. It is a desire for eros which motivates this book. My concern is to recover the peculiar power of traditional religious images. More particularly, what I seek is a truly trinitarian way to understand the mystery of the Trinity.

The mythopoetic argument moves through the numbered chapters, one through six. Part 1 (chaps. 1–2) attempts to recover the images which lie dormant in the theological ideas of the Trinity, and to discover the likenesses of these images to psychological life. Part 2 (chaps. 3–4) presses the trinitarian images back and down into the depths of mythic imagination. Part 3 (chaps. 5–6) displays a poetics of the mytho-theology of the Trinity, noting what has become of the images of the trinitarian idea in the literary sensibility of our own time.

Each of these three steps is focused in an Interlude, where the remembering, contemplating, and loving are grounded in actual case studies. The particular instance in part 1 is the depth psychology of Freud and Jung. In part 2, the examples are from philosophy, the social sciences, and literary theory. The modern theater of Harold Pinter provides the realistic witness in part 3 that the trinitarian perspective is alive and well here and now. Throughout, the aim is to demonstrate that theological idea, mythic image, and poetic metaphor are actually at work in the perspectives and paradigms of thinking and sensing in our time.

James Joyce once wrote: "Wipe your glosses with what you know!"[25] Such is the intuition of a theology learned from secular culture and from the deep self.

The doctrines and teachings of theology—the ways of imagining—lie close. "Closer to you than your jugular vein," says the Koran. And there is Augustine's discovery: "I had sought Thee without, but Thou wert within, closer to me than I was to myself."

So, perhaps, with the Trinity . . .

# PART ONE

# REMEMBERING THE TRINITY

# 1

## IMAGES AND
## FANTASIES HIDDEN IN
## RELIGIOUS TRADITIONS
### Theological Formulae of the Trinity

This work on the Trinity is not a work in the field of Christian theology only, since trinitarian formulae appear not only in the Christian tradition but in many, if not all, of the world's religious traditions. Nor is this a work in the field of religions only, since there is something ineluctably trinitarian about human experience in general.

This sense has been intuited and expressed by many, including Russian theologian Nicholas Berdyaev who has written:

> Wherever there is life there is the mystery of "three-in-oneness" . . . The meeting of one with another is always resolved in a third. The one and the other come to unity, not in duality, but in trinity: in the third (person) they discover their common content, their goal. Being would be in a condition of indifference . . . if there were only one. It would be hopelessly torn and divided if there were only two. Being discloses its meaning . . . while remaining in unity, because there are three. Such is the nature of being, the primal fact of its life.[1]

Similarly, Paul Tillich observed, "If we ask why, in spite of . . . openness to different numbers, the number three has prevailed, it seems most probably that the three corresponds to the intrinsic dialectics of experienced life."[2] This twentieth-century sensibility is but a recent echo of earlier witness by Jacob Boehme ("No place or position can be found or conceived where the . . . Trinity is not present and in every being; but hidden as the essence of it"),[3] Meister Eckhart ("The Trinity is the heart of . . . human nature"),[4] and Augustine ("A reflection of the Trinity is to be found in every creature").[5] What these few have expressed will be amplified many times over as our argument proceeds, and the testimony will by no means be confined to thinkers of a religious stripe.

The Trinity is human. Indeed, it is "all too human" (Nietzsche). But human experience *as* trinitarian is already a human experiencing that is being viewed through religious image, metaphor, and trope. To remember trinitarian formulations in the history of religions is to re-member the human in a particular way; it is to put together what is dismembered in living reality according to a specifically meaningful vision.

To be sure, the special religious image called by the name Trinity has received a decisive expression in Christian tradition, a tradition which has not only spoken trinitarianly, like so many others, but which has preeminently insisted — in word, if not always in deed — upon the fact that ultimate reality, or reality seen ultimately, is fundamentally trinitarian. It is, therefore, particularly to Christian formulae that this book attends, but without any intention of exclusiveness. This is why one may have the impression that this is a book in Christian theology, which would be true and, at the same time, not true.

Before exploring in detail the decisive Christian formula of the Trinity and the human fantasies which are secreted within it, we would do well to demonstrate concretely what has already been asserted: that trinitarian formulae appear in many, if not all, of the world's religious traditions. It is not in any way a claim of this study to be a compendious survey of an image in the world's religions. This is not a comparative enterprise, not *Stoffgeschichte* (a history of stuff). Nonetheless, an archetypal theology implies a work of re-membering which is very large in scope; it is a work which can never be completed in a single work, in a single time, or by a single person. Christian theological remembering can function and often has functioned to dismember, splitting Athens from Jerusalem, West from East, till never can they again meet. So it is that I begin concretely, not only with an affirmation of the fundamental humanness of the Trinity, but also religiously beyond the pale of Christianity altogether.

Since a motif-history in world religions is not my main purpose, it is all the more to the good that numerous authors have already achieved what I wish at the outset to demonstrate. It can serve our purpose here merely to mention the results of their labors, and then to specify a few samples which may stand for the whole.

Raymond Pannikar has shown philosophically the similarity of the

Christian notion of the Trinity to certain religious structures in Hinduism. His book, *The Trinity and World Religions*,[6] is a "meditation" which, using a South Asian terminology and Christian formulae side by side, compares three fundamental ways of being religious with the structure of ultimate reality. *Karmamarga* (the way of religious action in life) implies, according to Pannikar's idea, an imagined god who must be commanding such action. To imagine such a power is to have an icon, an image of ultimacy; it is iconolatry, though not necessarily idolatry. *Bhaktimarga* (the way of devotion and compassion) is different. It marks the "normal blossoming of the dimension of religious personality," a "mutual acceptance and communication" between persons. *Jnanamarga* (the way of knowledge and contemplation) leads the person to a sense of the "non-dual" (*advaita*) nature of god (*Brahman*) and the self (*Atman*), thus revealing the deepest religious mystery — that transcendence and immanence are not ultimately opposed. The source *super omnes* (above all); the person and being *per omnia* (through all); and the spirit *in omnibus* (in all) — this trinity corresponds, in Pannikar's view, to these three ways of being religious.

It is also the trinitarian structure of Hinduism which is linked, by Georges Dumézil, to a phenomenology of the religions of ancient Rome and northern Europe.[7] Dumézil's tripartite ideology and hermeneutic are well known in academic circles of the history of religions. He sees similar functions played by Jupiter, Mars, and Quirinius in Roman myth, Odinn, Thor, and Freyr in northern European myth, and Mitra-Varuna, Indra, and Nasatya in South Asia. This typology is built upon a view of the social classes of *brahman*, *kshatriya*, and *vaisya*. They point to political functions of sovereignty (magical and judicial aspects of life), physical power and bravery (warrior life), and fertility and economic prosperity (nourishment and providing for the well-being of all).

Where Pannikar examines piety philosophically and Dumézil interprets religion sociologically, a third phenomenologist, Gerardus Van der Leeuw, proceeds historically by way of motifs and images. Working in encyclopaedic fashion, Van der Leeuw finds a triad of ultimate reality in the religions of Egypt (Osiris, Isis, Horus); ancient Greece (the theogony of Ouranos, Kronos, and Zeus); the ancient Near East (Attis, Ishtar, and Tammuz); and India (the *trimurti* of Brahma, Rudra, and Vishnu).[8]

To the philosopher, sociologist, and historian may be added the literary critic, Philip Wheelwright, who, in a study of the language and literature of symbolism, gives an analysis of what he terms "the primal triad."[9] Wheelwright finds the basis of trinitarian religious symbology in biology (the family pattern of father, mother, child) and in the geometry of human thought patterns (the beginning, middle, and end of linear structure; and the down-here/earth, up-there/sky, and in-between/atmosphere). It is into these modes of the "triadic archetype," as he calls it, that Wheelwright places Egyptian, Greek, Zoroastrian, Hindu, and Buddhist, not to mention Christian, images and ideas.

That these four works are by a philosopher, a sociologist, a historian, and a literary critic could lead one to assume that the universal imagery of three in religions of the world correlates with several different aspects of humanness — the mental life by which one *thinks* of religious piety (philosophy and literature), and the ethical and ritualistic manner in which one *behaves* (sociology and history), each aspect amenable to being experienced as if in three parts which, if not one, at least may be seen as belonging together intimately in life.

Of course, many more examples could be given. In chapter 3, specific Greek mythological modes of trinity will be examined in order to deepen the background of Christian ideas. In chapter 4, the Christian notions will be amplified by way of Gnosticism, Renaissance thought, Neoplatonism, and alchemy, which, if not non-Christian, have at least been marginal to dominant Christian teaching and understanding. These later chapters will therefore be additional testimony to the grand religious scope of trinitarian thinking. Suffice it for the initial purposes of this chapter simply to give three further concrete examples of trinity where, from Christian perspective, it may not have been expected.

Frank Reynolds has called the doctrine of the Trikaya (three bodies) in both Mahayana and Theravada Buddhism of South Asia a "neglected" doctrine, perhaps just as neglected as the Trinity in Western Christendom.[10] This doctrine testifies from ancient times to the one Buddha as having three "bodies"— the *Dharmakaya* (body of the essence) which is absolute, formless, and eternal; the *Nirmanakaya* (body of historical manifestation) which has been particularly manifest in the incarnation of Gotama Siddhartha; and the *Sambhoyakaya* (body of bliss) which stands between the other two as their experiential spiritual link. These bodies may correspond, as Richard Pilgrim has argued compellingly, to the early Indian cosmology of celestial heaven, terrestrial earth, and the atmosphere between; or to the traditional Hindu notion of *cit* = consciousness itself, *sat* = existential manifestation of consciousness itself, and *ananda* = bliss or spiritual power.

The doctrine of the Trikaya is important, if neglected, in Buddhist theology. It describes the modalities of ultimate reality (the Buddhanature). On the face of it, the formal parallel to the idea of the Trinity in Christian theology is hard to miss — essential father, his historical manifestation in the son, and the spirit between the other two serving as their connection and their experiential power in actual religious life. It would seem that a theology of trinity is not unique to Christianity.

But even if it is not so surprising to discover a trinity "theology" in a so-called atheistic religion of the Orient, one nonetheless may not have expected to find it, as one does, in the radical monotheistic tradition of Judaism.

It is in the iconography of iconoclastic Jewish monotheism that the French scholar W. L. Dulière documents, in painstaking fashion, a trinitarian sense of divinity. Dulière's massive volume is titled *From the Dyad to Unity by Way of the Triad*,[11] and his argument, precisely expressed by this title, is that one can see a development of notions of the Deity in the history of the Jewish religion if one examines its religious art.

The first stage in the development of theological ideas in art is symbolized by the representation of a pair of cherubim with an abstract design between them (figure 1). Or, to give another of the many examples utilized by Dulière, one may find two animals, symbolizing a divine vision, linked by one head (figures 2, 3, 4). The animals in the images of this period are often calves or winged bulls. As religious art evolves, these cherubim figures are progressively humanized, but typically some bestial elements, such as horns or wings, remain.

The next stage, according to Dulière's analysis of the materials, is typified by a triad — a triad which will ultimately lead to a unity — wherein the bestial figure is a third factor between the other two

Figure 1

Figure 2

Figure 3

Figure 4

Figure 5

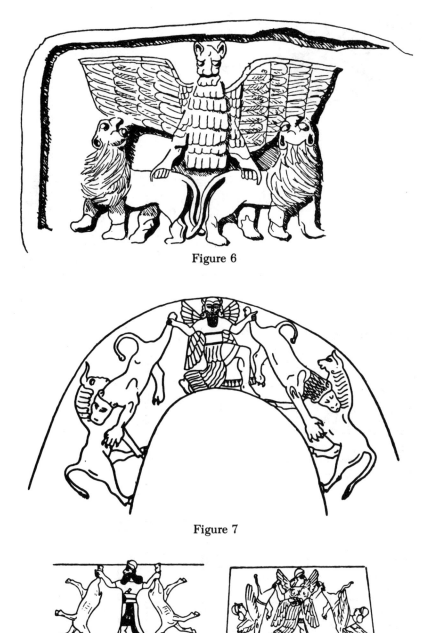

Figure 6

Figure 7

Figure 8

Figure 9

Figure 10

Figure 11

Figure 12

which have now become recognizably human (figure 5). Gradually the animal in the center becomes more dominant and more domineering (figure 6). Next, this central figure is humanized and pictured as aggressively and violently willing the destruction of the other two, which are now pictured as pagan beasts (figures 7, 8). Until, finally, we are left with the one in the center alone (figure 9). This one, however, still carries the mark of threeness, indicated here by the two outstretched hands. After examining the history of the religious art of Judaism, it is not difficult, Dulière argues, to see that the trinity of the unity is still implicated.

Furthermore, Dulière notes, the iconography of the Christian trinitarian tradition shows a similar pattern (figures 10, 11, 12).

Surely, even those who are not compelled by Dulière's developmental argument, in spite of whatever preconceptions about Jewish monotheism they may have, will find the pictorial data enlightening. The image of threeness seems somehow fundamentally given. It is an image basic to even iconoclastic traditions which are shy about picturing God—not only Judaism but also Zen.

It would certainly be out of harmony with the spirit of Japanese Zen to attempt to interpret Sengai's brush painting. At the very least, it would not be in keeping with the Zen-spirit to analyze it in the way that Dulière explains Jewish art. But a koan may, nonetheless, be to the point.

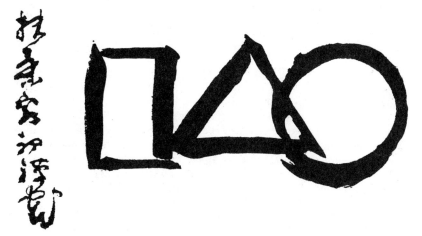

CIRCLE, TRIANGLE, AND SQUARE, by Sengai (1750–1837)

The *Mumonkan* was originally published in China toward the end of the southern Sung dynasty in about the thirteenth century. It is a collection of forty-eight koans which have accumulated, over the years, many *teisho* or interpretations. One of the most difficult of the koans is the following:

> The National Teacher called to his attendant three times, and the attendant answered three times. The National Teacher said, "I thought I had transgressed against you, but you too had transgressed against me."[12]

A twentieth-century master, Zenkei Shibyama, reports one traditional commentary in the form of yet another koan:

> Repeatedly she calls out, "Oh, Shogyoku!"
> It is for no other purpose
> Than that her lover
> May recognize her voice.[13]

Shibyama explains that it would not be in the spirit of Zen for one human being to call out to another so as to achieve some purpose with that person. It would be a transgression, one person using another. But the calling with Zen no-mind and the response of the other with Zen no-mind has the function of uniting the two in Buddha oneness. Distinctions between self and other, between subject and object are overcome, as they are between a parent and child when the parent speaks so that only the child knows of the loving care and presence, or as they are between lovers who are one even while individually two. Shibyama writes, "If you take up a flower, you yourself are a flower."[14] And then he concludes by saying:

> To call the Truth "it" is already staining it. There is no such distinction as subject and object in the Truth. It has neither form nor name. If I call out "Oshin!" I have already committed the transgression of giving a false name to the unnamable. And if you answer "Yes, Master" to my calling a false name, you have certainly transgressed against me [since we are One in our Buddha-natures, just as two persons are one in Love, Love being a "third" which is unnamable since it is a no-thing]. This is what the old Master means. The father well understands his son. This transgression of the father and the son in Oneness beautifully depicts the characteristic of Zen.[15]

Can one say less as a Christian (or more, for that matter?) than that the Father and the Son are one trinitarianly in the third, which is Spirit, and therefore a *nada*, a no-thing?

In a text on the Zen art of flower arranging, Shibyama writes:

> Yesterday, the heart of a demon
> This morning, the face of a Bodhisattva.
> A demon and a Bodhisattva —
> No distinction is existent.

> A butcher and a Buddha's disciple, nature and art, they are neither one
> nor two. Here we come to the inexpressible, and from this exquisite
> point true religion and true art shines out with eternal brilliance. . . .
> Zen man Rikyu once said, "In arranging flowers for a small room, one
> flower, or two, of single color, is to be lightly arranged." I like this
> remark very much. The word "lightly" is not light at all; in this one
> word we can detect . . . Zen insight. . . . When it comes to this point,
> there is no distinction between religion and art. They are identified;
> they are neither one nor two.[16]

So, are they then a third? Of course, and of course not. Concerning
the third one may not speak, for it is no-thing, since it is everything.
This may be indeed why St. Augustine said, "Who can understand
the omnipotent Trinity? And yet who does not speak about it, if
indeed it is of it that he speaks? Rare is the soul who, when he speaks
of it, also knows of what he speaks."[17] It is in this context of Zen, and
in those of Judaism and Indian Buddhism, not to mention the many
other religions to which allusions have already been made, that one
comes to the Christian notion of the Trinity.

Certainly it would be an easy matter to list further instances of
threeness in world religions. But in the specific examples we have
given, as in Christian doctrine, it is divinity or ultimate reality (truth
in the Zen tradition) which is imagined triangularly, as if it were
indeed the case, as Virgil has written, that "God rejoices in odd
numbers"[18] generally, and particularly in the number three, as
Marsilio Ficino observed, saying, "The Pythagorean philosophers
believed that a trinity was the measure of everything, for the reason,
I think, that God governs things in threes."[19]

Yet, although the testimony may seem universal, it has been particularly the Christian religious tradition that has been stubborn about
insisting on the threeness of the one Divine Reality. Therefore, it is
in a Christian theology, where so many words have been spilled over
this matter and where so many tomes have troubled over its meaning,
that we seek an articulation of the "logic" of what everywhere is

intuited, noting at the outset that the One is unspeakable and that the Third which makes the Two cohere is unnameable and that three-in-oneness is illogical already on the face of it.

Indeed, it was Tertullian (also noted for saying *credo quia absurdum est*, I believe because it is absurd) who was the first to have spoken of God as Trinity. At the beginning of the third century he wrote, "Let us preserve the mystery of the divine economy (*oikonomia, dispensatio*) which disposes the unity into trinity, the Father, the Son and the Holy Spirit, three not in essence but in grade, not in substance but in form."[20] Tertullian's formula, which became the formula for the Western church, was *una substantia, tres personae* (one substance, three persons). As opposed to this Latin form, Hippolytus and subsequently the Eastern church said, *mian ousian, treis hypostaseis* (one essence, three substances).

Not only is there the problem of affirming that one is three and three is one, but also there is the awkwardness that in Greek the words *hypostasis* and *ousia* were originally synonyms,[21] making the Greek formula sound as if it says, "one essence but three essences." There is further the problem of why in the East "substance" (Greek *hypostasis*) is three whereas in the West "substance" (Latin *substantia*) is one. All of this confuses not only modern ears; Augustine complained in his work *On the Trinity* (*De Trinitate*) that he could not tell the difference between an *ousia* and a *hypostasis*.[22]

But in spite of these difficulties the testimony and its intuition stuck. The so-called Athanasian Creed, also known as the *Symbolum quicumque* (whoever would be saved), has this formulation: "Now the Catholic Faith is this: That we worship one God in Trinity, and Trinity in Unity, neither confounding the Persons nor dividing the substance. . . . So that in all ways . . . both the Trinity is to be worshipped in Unity, and the Unity in Trinity." And then the creed concludes: "He, therefore, that would be saved, let him think thus of the Trinity."[23] This formulation persisted, so that in 553, the anathemas of the Second Council of Constantinople, the Fifth Ecumenical Council, read: "If anyone does not confess one nature or substance, one power and authority, of Father and Son and Holy Spirit, consubstantial Trinity, one Deity worshipped in three *hypostases* or persons, let him be anathema."[24]

There must be a reason deeper than church politics for the staying power of these formulae that are not so unlike others we have noted in other times and traditions. By attending carefully to the *language* as it is given in Christian theological formulae, we may be able to tease out the important fantasies hidden so deeply within the universal religious intuition concealing ultimate reality.

There is implied in the trinitarian formulae a notion that ultimately (for this is language about God) things which seem to be one are, on closer attention, actually three. We are asked by this idea, as Augustine puts it in the *Confessions,* to "see the trinity of unity."[25] Stated another way, one may say that when two things, like a father and a son, seem to be one, there will be a third factor that is the spirit of the relationship. Though this haunting factor be a third it is nonetheless responsible for the unity of the other two. When two seem one, there is ultimately in the transpersonal "economy" a third. Or, there is a third which is an ultimate and transpersonal factor working to connect the two. This seems the case not only in Christian formulae but also in the instances we have cited from Buddhism, Judaism, and Zen.

But this third is somehow not quite like the other two. There are Father and Son, says the Christian formula. But the Third is a ghost. The first two are metaphors of family relationships. To continue the symbolism consistently one might have expected father, son, mother; or father, son, daughter; or father, son, grandfather; or father, son, cousin. But this is not the fantasy of the Christian view. Rather we are presented with a view of things unified by (a) being of the same sex, homoerotic or homosexual, and (b) containing a third which is, though like the others in gender and sexuality, nonetheless different in kind — being a ghost, a spirit, a shade, a soul, an image or *eidolon.* The homoerotic fantasy of the Trinity is likely not about sex or social relationships understood literally. Rather, it is a *symbolum* or metaphor which imagines that things belonging together in a constellating and configuring way are *like* each other rather than unlike. This is what made for the fuss in Christian history over the words *homoousian* (of the same substance) and *homoiousian* (of like substance). Yet, in spite of this dogged focus on similitude and sameness, the likeness of the two is somehow guaranteed by the third "likeness" which, though indeed belonging with the other two, is not like them in the same way in which they are like each other.

There is yet another dimension to the fantasy of the trinitarian formulae. Not only are we asked to view the trinity of unity ghosted by
a third, but we are also to look for the "unity of trinity,"[26] as if when
things appear to be triangular or to come to us in threesomes, however disjunct and awkward the situation may seem, they *ultimately*
belong together as if one. Augustine in the *Enchiridion* writes,
"When any one of the three is named in connection with some action,
the whole Trinity is to be understood as involved,"[27] as if any one of
any threesome involves every member of the triangle.

Now what is this trinitarian fantasia all about? If it were simply
a mathematical matter, a conundrum with numbers for philosophers
and mathematicians to puzzle over, why would the Christian tradition, not to mention others, have so insisted upon it and fought over
it? And in spite of its insistence on the Trinity, why would that same
tradition have so muted the concept, rarely teaching it, and remain-
ing for the most part binitarian, often defending itself against the
trinitarian idea by stressing only the doctrines of God and Christ?

The suggestion has been made by some through the years that such
questions as these confound people because the Trinity has been mis-
*placed*. Its power and reality have been missed, they have argued, by
attempts to locate the referent of the Trinity in an other world.
Already we have noted that Augustine spoke of the *vestigia trinitatis*
in everyday life, rather than in some metaphysical site. There are
"traces of the Trinity," he observed, in all things.[28] Jacob Boehme also
has been cited: "No place or position can be found or conceived
where the spirit of the Trinity is not present and in every being; but
hidden as the essence of it."[29]

More particularly, the problem seems to be that we have tended to
look for the Trinity in some transcendental locale, some supernaturalistic place, wholly other, as if we were carefully defending
against what we might be able to learn if we discovered the Trinity
within the self's own experience here and now. In his work *On True
Religion*, Augustine writes, "Do not go abroad. Return within yourself. In the inward man dwells the truth."[30] And again, he wrote concerning the Divine Reality: "Thou wast within and I was without,
and I sought Thee out there. . . . Thou wast with me, but I was not
with Thee."[31]

Some will object, of course. They will say that to follow the

Augustinian clue is to psychologize the divine, reducing the divine to the human. But this is not necessarily the case at all. Between the dogmatic tendency to view God as "wholly other" and the pietistic tendency to see God in human experience there is a third way, the imaginal way described in the introduction.

Learning theology in the self is not the same as attempting to learn theology in the so-called ego. It is not a case of some narcissistic or subjectivistic introspection that expects to find theological truths in behavior or in some sense of I, me, or mine. A danger in the approach this book takes is, to be sure, that some persons will imagine the uncanny discovery of likenesses between the perennial and enduring mythic formulae of religions and the everyday experiences of humankind as a psychologism or a romanticism. But the opportunity in the danger is that, far from psychologizing theology, far from humanizing the divine, one may begin to see persons from other than an ego-psychological perspective, now under the aegis of religious and mythic images, theologizing the self and so amplifying life rather than reducing religion.

All the more, then, it would not be surprising to discover in contemporary depth (as opposed to behavioral and ego) psychology, the ancient trinitarian insight and structure that is so universally persistent in religions and is expressed so articulately in the images—the fantasies and intuitions—of Christianity. That this is indeed the case we will pause to observe in the following interlude before continuing to remember the Trinity following the Augustinian clue.

Interlude

# FREUD AND JUNG
## The Trinity in
## Modern Depth Psychology

In 1966 Norman O. Brown, a scholar and teacher of Greek classics, wrote a remarkable work, frankly Freudian, but not, for that matter, less theological. *Love's Body* contained a chapter entitled "Trinity" which was followed by one called "Unity." That something theological was implied seemed clear from both the constant references to religion and the chapter headings. But by Trinity Brown also — and perhaps preeminently — meant something psychological, as if, in trinitarian perspective, theology and psychology were one in "love's body." Brown wrote:

> The parents in coitus make one flesh; not a juxtaposition of two separatenesses, but a genuine Two-in-One, incorporated; making one corporate body.[1]

The "inner eye" which sees the parental "primal scene" this way is, of course, in a depth-psychological perspective, that of the child. Thus, in some fundamentally deep way, the two-in-one are three-in-one: a triangle whose mythic and psychic name is, by one accounting, Oedipus.

Freud, however, did not limit himself to the Oedipal theme when discussing the profoundly triangular nature of the self. In 1913, drawing on material from mythology, folk tales, and world literature, he published an essay titled "The Theme of the Three Caskets." In it, Freud observed that

> the shepherd Paris has to choose between three goddesses, of whom he declares the third [Aphrodite] to be the fairest. Cinderella is another such youngest, and is preferred by the prince to the two elder sisters;

Psyche in the tale of Apuleius is the youngest and fairest of the three sisters; on the one hand, she becomes human and is revered as Aphrodite, on the other she is treated by the goddess as Cinderella was treated by her stepmother and has to sort a heap of mixed seeds, which she accomplishes with the help of little creatures (doves for Cinderella, ants for Psyche).[2]

And then Freud notes that "anyone who cared to look more closely into the material could undoubtedly discover other versions of the same idea in which the same essential features had been retained."[3]

Freud wonders about this motif which has so endured in human expression. "Who," he asks, "are these three sisters and why must the choice fall on the third?" He imagines that "if we could answer this question, we should be in possession of the solution we are seeking." And then he notes that "this surpassing third has in several instances certain peculiar qualities . . . that seem to be tending toward some kind of unity."[4] In fact, for Freud, at least early in his work, it is a third aspect of the structure of the self — be it id, death, eros, mother, child — which serves to unify other warring dualities, such as ego and superego, individual instincts and collective responsibility, or the ambivalence of love and hate. As Christine Downing has shown, "Freud refers often to the importance of the 'third' in provoking psychic life."[5]

In her book, *The Goddess*, Downing explains Freud's point.

The dyad, whether it unites mother and infant or husband and wife, tends to be static. It is often characterized more by fusion than by genuine relating; the arrival of the third (father or mistress) forces differentiation, change, movement.[6]

Downing's examples (mother and child, husband and wife) seem to refer to social rather than to psychological experience. Freud's insight about the triangular nature of the *deep* self — the Oedipal structure of the development of the psyche, or the super-ego/ego/id structure of the nature of the psyche — is theoretical, and it belongs to fantasy rather than to empirical reality. The self is not composed of an actual historical father and an actual historical mother and an actual historical child. Rather, it is constituted by "screen memories"— father-image, mother-image, and child-image. Though it may well be the case (see Downing's richly illustrated point) that psychic fantasies will be acted out in everyday behaviors, trinitarian psychology, like trinitarian theology, refers finally to *ultimate* reality, the deep self, the fantastical and mythic. When a person interprets a life-situation as Oedipal or as a three sisters situation or as a Zeus-Hera-Nymph triangle, it *is* an interpretation. And interpretation comes, usually unconsciously, from within the self — indeed, from within a triangled self. We see and sense things triangularly because we are trinities. Freud's is a *depth* psychology, not a behavioral psychology or ego psychology; nor is it a sociology of everyday life.

It was one of Freud's great discoveries that the self is at base fantastical. He wrote to his friend, Wilhelm Fliess, in 1897, admitting that when patients spoke of their erotic Oedipal situations with their parents he had evidence to show that such relationships had not been literally based in the persons' actual histories.[7] Freud's "proposal," as he called it in his lectures to the medical school in Vienna during the winter semester of 1916–1917, was "that we should equate phantasy and reality."[8] The trinity of psychoanalysis is "primal fantasy."[9]

This point is stressed here because, as we shall see in the next chapter, to lose the sense of Freud's psychoanalytic "proposal," as so many in the study of religion have done, is to lose an opportunity for sensing the depth of the theological notion of the Trinity. When the deeper sense is missing the notion becomes mere dogma or mere piety, rather than the rich imaginal structure it is in the thinking of Augustine, for example.

Nor do theologians alone lose the radical sense of Freud's discovery; psychoanalysts waffle as well. For example, the transactional analysis of Eric Berne continues the psychoanalytic insight concerning threeness in psychology.[10] The fundamental triad is said to be parent-child-adult. For the most part in the "games people play," they hide their ulterior motives while trying to win something or other, and parade parentally in relation to others, appearing to care for or to lord it over the others; or, on the other hand, they pout and shrink in childishness, hoping that boss or spouse or government or religion will provide for them. Like some Hegelian pendulum or waddling psychic duck, selves swing back and forth between behaviors of parent and child, but aim, hopefully, for a more mature "game-free" life, the life of an adult who recognizes, but does not act out, the parent and the child within the self.

This triadic psychology seems to be on the borderline between behavior (acting out) and fantasy (the parent and child within). But its view tempts one to depart from the Freudian depths of self. It tends toward sociology, if not toward a new pseudo-Protestant, California morality, as in Stephen Karpman's "drama triangle."[11]

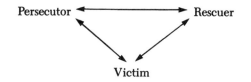

Persecutor ←————————→ Rescuer

Victim

Each person, according to Karpman's scheme, enters the script of the drama in each of the scenes of life in one of the three main roles, with another actual person (not another aspect of the self) in one of the other roles. When a crisis occurs, there is a switch. Eric Berne gives an example:

> During marriage, for example, the husband is the persecutor and the wife plays the part of the victim. Once a divorce complaint is filed, these roles are reversed: the wife becomes the persecutor, and the husband the victim, while his lawyer and her lawyer play the part of competing rescuers.[12]

Not only this example, but the theory itself is sociological and behavioral, having to do with the actions of egos. It is a long way from Freud's vision and his proposal; further away, even, than was C. G. Jung, whom history records as having been Freud's antagonist.

Jung, like Freud, struggled with the fantasy of a trinitarian self. For Freud, the wrestling began, as Norman O. Brown and others have noted,[13] late in life, at the time of the publication of *Beyond the Pleasure Principle*. Freud came to see the profoundly dualistic nature of the self—ego against id, child against parents, life against death, love against hate. He searched for the third to hold the self together. Monotheism was the name he gave to it in his last book. But a third factor evaded him. Oedipus gave way to Moses and Empedocles. And, in an essay which asked whether therapy is "terminable or interminable," Freud concluded his life's work pessimistically, as Brown notes.[14] A trinitarian psychology finally failed him because the nature of whatever third there might be was that of "ghost" or "phantasm." He could not put his finger on it. It is not easy to equate fantasy with reality.

The story of Jung's similar struggle with and against the Trinity is instructive in the context of Freud's shift to a perspective of instinctual dualism in later life. Like the old man Freud, the old man Jung wondered about a "transcendent function," an *unus mundus*, which could give psychological reality in actual life to a self which is fundamentally a *complexio oppositorum* (a warring of oppositions) — ego and shadow, *anima* (feminine soul) and *animus* (masculine spirit), eros (tendency to connect) and logos (tendency to differentiate). Jung, like Freud, referred to this life-dilemma as the problem of "monotheism."[15]

For Jung, the question of the third in a person's psychology has to do with whether the third in the psychic life is the uniting factor or whether it makes an imbalance which itself needs a fourth for wholeness. This theoretical psychological problem focused itself concretely for Jung in the meaning of the theological symbol of the Trinity, and his difficulties with the Trinity began early.

A problem between Jung and his father concerning the Trinity, and Jung's general suspicion that theologians and philosophers did not know the least thing about the Trinity recurred in 1940 when Jung was over sixty. The place was the Eranos Conference in Ascona, Switzerland. Because of political events in Europe, only one lecture was announced and that by Andreas Speiser, a professor of mathematics from the University of Zurich. The topic was "The Platonic Doctrine of the Unknown God and the Christian Trinity." Jung listened to the lecture and during that afternoon he retired into the garden, asking for a Bible and some time to reflect. The next day he improvised a lecture entitled "On the Psychology of the Trinity."

Jung said that "we must distinguish between the logical idea and a psychological reality of the Trinity. . . . The platonic formula of the third [as necessary for an understanding of the relationship between any two distinct factors[16]] is certainly the last word in logical perspective, but psychologically it is certainly not, since the psychological reality [of a third] forces itself upon us in a fearful and disturbing manner. . . . Logic says: *tertium non datur* [a third is not given]. But life, and especially soul-life witnesses to the connections of doubleness always by a third which appears as incommensurable and paradoxical."[17] What is not given and is refused by philosophical logic, Jung said, echoing Freud's sentiment, is the *Tiefen der Seele* (the depths of soul) in human experience.[18] Jung said straightforwardly, "Father and Son are linked in Soul."[19] And then he concluded his improvised lecture with the words, "We are pointing towards a mystery of inner experience which borders us but remains silent."[20]

Jung worked and reworked this improvisation over the next seven years, and in 1948 it appeared under the cautious title, "An Attempt at a Psychological Presentation of the Dogma of the Trinity."[21] His caution is also felt in a letter Jung wrote to H. G. Baynes in the May following the Eranos lecture. "I seem to be dealing," Jung confided to Baynes, "more and more with subjects not suitable for public discussion (. . . Trinity)."[22] In another letter four years later, Jung joined the church father, Tertullian, in calling the Trinity an "impossible idea,"[23] continuing thereby to stress the offensive and paradoxical nature of the Trinity. Writing to the Roman Catholic scholar, Victor White, in 1946, still two years before the published version of the essay, Jung said, "I must make up my mind to tackle my dangerous paper about the psychology of the Holy Trinity."[24]

But the Eranos lecture and the aftermath is not all there is to the Jungian story. Jung often wrote of his irritation at the ways in which professors and theologians interpreted the Trinity, likening their feeble attempts to a situation in the life of the Swiss national saint, Brother Nicholas of Flue.[25] Nicholas had had a vision of a terrifying face that he identified as the face of God—very much as Jung had identified one of his own early dreams as referring to God's terrifying aspect.[26] But in Nicholas's case the vision was interpreted by the church from the point of view of a rationalistic and dogmatic theology. The church's traditional reading called Nicholas's vision a pious sensing of the Holy Trinity, saying nothing about its negative aspect. In 1957, Jung wrote in a letter: "Actually after this vision Nicholas should have preached, 'God is terrible.' But he believed the interpretation instead of the immediate experience."[27] The point is that our theological interpretations of the Trinity have served to soften the "dangerousness" and offensiveness of this doctrine, and hence have rendered it either incomprehensible or banal.[28]

The result of Jung's reaction to this banalizing theological tradition has been to lead many Jungians and students of Jung to imagine that he dismissed the trinitarian notion of the self in favor of the quaternarian view. But Jung's actual writings show the matter to be more complicated. Indeed, he did argue from time to time that the appearance of three of this or that in a dream or fantasy indicated an incomplete "mandala" (*i.e.*, a self which is still developing and has an inferior and unconscious side which needs recognition and acceptance). But this is not Jung's only view — at least, according to his writings. Indeed, one may discern three different dimensions to his thinking in the matter of the triadic self.

Early in his psychological practice, Jung recognized that whenever a trinity emerges in a patient's dream, fantasy, or behavior, it is a matter of eros or sexual connections, no matter what the patient might think or say. Jung believed such situations were most appropriately symbolized, not by Oedipus, but by Eros, Dionysos, Priapus, and Phales, who were viewed as apt archetypal expressions of the sensuous triangles that were deeply basic to the self.[29] These were structures of self honored in themselves.

Later, however, Jung began to believe something different. Based still on his therapeutic practice (not to mention his own psychological experiences), Jung intuited that when images of threeness arise in the self, some fourth may be lacking. He referred to this situation of the self as a "disturbed mandala," and his negative view of three typically appears during this middle part of his life.[30]

After Jung began to study alchemy, however, his view concerning threeness became less one-sided. He often observed in the symbology of the most profound regions of the self that a trinity is deepened not by some fourth factor of the self but rather by what Jung called an *umbra trinitatis*, a shadow of trinity, chthonic threesome, or lower triad. The so-called dark side of an ultimate reality (self or God) that is trinitarian is not a fourth factor (devil or anima) but is, rather, to give just one example, a three-headed animal.[31]

During this third period in Jung's writing, there appeared frequent positive prognoses about threeness in regard to the self, as long, of course, as the threeness is viewed deeply, including in its bestial and other dangerous aspects, rather than dogmatically or pietistically. For example, citing Virgil, Jung wrote, "God prefers odd numbers."[32] And he quoted the *Aurora consurgens*: "All perfection consisteth in the number three."[33] Jung also cited in psychological perspective a portion of one of the Christian creeds: "He that would be saved [*i.e.*, healed], let him think on Trinity."[34] By no means was this psychologist *only* negative about the Trinity. Indeed, he called it "the most sacred of all dogmatic symbols."[35]

Nor has this religious image disappeared from the psychology of Jungians, though — as in the case of the Freudians — there is some waffling on whether the metaphor of the Trinity belongs to the deep self, as in the cases of Jung and Freud, or to the ego and its behaviors. A few examples will make the point.

Edward Edinger, in his book *Ego and Archetype,* devotes a chapter to the trinity archetype. He notes that Jung is best known for his theory about the quaternity of a balanced self, but that it may be reported from clinical practice that the image of threeness is often encountered in work with persons for whom it is not a case of an "incomplete or amputated quaternity." Edinger notes that in at least one place Jung spoke of the Trinity as a symbol of psychological development (*i.e.,* from being a child of a parent [father], to being parent of a child [son], to being a self alone with one's own soul [spirit]). Edinger reports that his own experience as an analyst agrees with that of Jung and that he thinks it is important to view the transformation and development of the self in terms of a triadic movement. By development Edinger means the history of the life of the ego. He says, in concluding the chapter, "Three is the number for egohood."[36]

Other Jungians seem also (like transactional Freudians) to place trinitarian images of self in the ego's social history. John Layard, for example, writes about "the third uniting factor" in terms of kinship theory from social anthropology. He says that

> the Christian dogma of the Trinity based on human kinship, in which the Holy Ghost is said to symbolize the love between Father and Son . . . is a dogma which as theologically stated . . . meant nothing to me until I thought of it in terms of kinship and the relationship between a human father and his son who are the prime rivals for the mother's love, so that the love between the father and the son would be something like "loving one's enemy."[37]

Similarly, it is the psychological dimension of the sociological relationship between the person in therapy and the analyst which is described by Wolfgang Giegerich in his article on "the third of the two." Giegerich analyzes the eros of the transference relationship — how the therapeutic dyad implies a third — in terms of the fantasy of the psychological theory which brings the two together and holds them together meaningfully.[38] Russell Lockhart, too, locates the third erotically in social relationships. He writes: "The third element like the sisters, the other woman, or other man, or mother-in-law, or job, or sex, or money, or children, or headache—all these are the third thing, that third element that comes between, in the between-space and inevitably so. It is the dynamic forcing depth."[39]

There is risk in giving personal illustration for psychological principle. What is risked is that a depth psychology will subtly shift to a behavioral or an ego psychology, and that the fantasies and images of the self, the interior dramas, the archetypal structures will be taken personally, making idols of the gods rather than transforming history into mystery. The danger lies in the potential for psychological literalization, a reduction of religious image to social event.

It is not that this is the intention of Edinger, Layard, Giegerich, or Lockhart. These Jungians invoke the Trinity for psychological purposes, attempting to remythologize experience rather than to demythologize religion. It is the same with Raphael Lopez-Pedraza and James Hillman.

Lopez writes about homoerotic relationships, noting that the homoerotic nature of the relation between two men, for example, is sustained by a fantasy. And the eros-fantasy, he observes, is a third in the relationship. Fantasy makes experience, rather than experience producing fantasies. Lopez cites Gabriele D'Annunzio to his point: "Love like all divine powers is not truly exalted except in a Trinity."[40] The third is not something literal, nor is the relationship between the two a some-*thing;* the whole is fantasy, spirit, soul, ghost—just like ideas, including religious ideas such as the Trinity.

Hillman seems to be on the same archetypal course. Not in one writing but in several, he has insisted upon the fundamentally triangular nature of psychological fantasy, what Lopez calls "trio psychology."[41] Hillman's metaphor is marriage, but he is speaking about the nature of the deep self. "The more rigidly we insist upon unity," he writes concerning the self, "the more will diversity constellate. The forsaken 'other' must inevitably appear: the repressed return." And then, he explains:

> The situation that occurs then is called a triangle, but the triangle [of behavior] is after the event [of the insistent fantasy of unity]. First the unity of marriage has constellated the 'other,' and only after the other has had his or her effect does the triangle appear. . . . The other releases

love from this psychic structure [of unity]. . . . The triangle necessarily releases a host of demons because it breaks up unity of psychic structure and its pairings of balance and compensation. The 'other' represents all 'others,' reminding us of the latently split nature of the psyche into multiples.[42]

In another work, Hillman emphasizes once again the richly diverse and polymorphous nature of our deep selves, saying, "So necessary is the triangular pattern that, even where two exist only for each other, a third will be imagined."[43] He gives examples of this fantasy spilling over into life, acted out, as when there is jealousy in a marriage over the relationship one of the partners has with an analyst. "The stage is set," Hillman observes, "for tragedy." But, he notes,

> Perhaps this is its necessity: the triangles of eros educate the psyche out of its girlish goodness, showing it the extent of its fantasies and testing its capacity. The triangle presents eros as the transcendent function creating out of two a third, which, like all impossible love, cannot be lived fully in actuality, so that the third comes as imaginal reality.[44]

In the experience of the fundamentally triangular nature of the deep self, the psyche is taught "by means of the triangle that the imaginal is most actual and the actual symbolic."[45] This is, of course, very near to Freud's proposal that "we should equate phantasy and reality."[46] It keeps the psychology in the realm of *depth*, and locates trinitarian thinking in *ultimate* reality. Psychologically, our triangles belong in the fantastical depths rather than to the ego. Theologically, it is God who is Trinity, not man.

The contemporary depth psychological insight gives common testimony—whether from the Freudian or Jungian side. The witness from therapeutic experience is that trinitarian fantasies have to do with love, with eros, with something sexual and sensual, with something that connects and binds into unity, whether in the intimacies of the dreams or visions of the self or in the messes of human behavior. So strong is this sense in depth psychology that when practitioners turn to theorizing, they are tempted to explain the sense in terms of experiences of actual love and examples of real sensuality, as if it were inevitable that the deepest sense of threeness would be spoken of in terms of love, marriage, and erotic entanglement.

The eros is real, and the nature of its reality is fantasy, a fantasy so potent that it can be expressed only in sensual ways. Perhaps this is what was meant by the term "transparency" in the writings of that remarkable precursor of contemporary depth psychology, Søren Kierkegaard, when he spoke about the nature of the self.

> Man is spirit. But what is spirit? Spirit is the self. But what is the self? The self is a relation which relates itself to its own self. . . . Man is a synthesis. . . . A synthesis is a relation between two factors. So regarded, man is not yet a self. In the relation between two, the relation is the third term. . . . By relating itself to its own self and by willing to be itself, the self is grounded transparently in the Power which posited it.[47]

This is to say: the self is a trinity if it is truly a whole self, which is a seeing through the self in its partialities, as if it were transparent, the deepest self and ultimate reality being triune images, each of the other.

# 2

# LIFE-LIKENESS
# AND UNLIKENESS
## The Trinity in Everyday Life

Prior to the interlude, we noted an argument made by St. Augustine, Jacob Boehme, and others. The argument had to do with a riddling matter: that while there is a universal tendency in the history of religions, and a particular insistence in Christianity, to refer to the one ultimate reality as a threesome, there is perduring bafflement about the meaning of this three-in-onement. Augustine suggested that we were bewildered because of a natural but misguided reasoning that looks in the wrong direction for the referent of this ultimate trinity; that is, we are bewildered by virtue of looking up and out, rather than down and in. Augustine's clue for a way of understanding is not uncommon in the ancient world. In the Gospel of Thomas, for example, there is the following expression of this theological perspective:

> Jesus said: Recognize what is in your sight, and that which is hidden from you will become plain to you. For there is nothing hidden which will not become manifest.[1]

And now we have seen that this procedural suggestion is found not only in the ancient world. Augustine's clue concerning remembering the *vestigia trinitatis* (tracings of the Trinity) within is curiously corroborated by secular depth psychology. But the question remains as to what the persistence of the notion of the Trinity from the ancient world to the modern means.

Augustine means his work *On the Trinity* to be biblically grounded. The scriptural key has, as it were, two notches: the notion from Genesis that persons are made in "the image of God" (*imago dei*), and the notion from St. Paul that humankind is able to know spiritual things "in the mirror" of everyday life (*per speculum*).[2]

41

Citing Rom. 1:20, Augustine affirms that "God's invisible attributes
. . . have been visible, ever since the world began . . . in the things
he has made."[3] So, if God is a Trinity, as Christians believe, then persons must be trinities, since they are made *imago dei*. It would follow
that one could know God in the mirror of self.[4]

Attempting to follow faithfully the saying of St. Paul, Augustine
indicates that he has written *On the Trinity*, not so the Trinity may
be seen "face to face," but so it may be seen "by likeness, in an enigma
or riddle" (*per speculum in aenigmatei*).[5] The mirror (*speculum*) of
self allows us to see an image or trace (*imago, vestigia*); and this
matter of the self then becomes the enigma or riddle of the Trinity
(*aenigmate*) which should be interpreted.[6] "Every such enigma," says
Augustine, "is an allegory."[7] And, as he argues, the allegory provides
a "likeness which is not to be found in the outer and sensible world,
but in the inner and mental one."[8] So, on this view, we may expect
to discover the mystery of the Divine Trinity in the mystery of the
deep self. Augustine calls this perspective "the hinge" of his starting
point, for, as he explains, "a place has first to be found where anything is to be sought" and in the self "we have . . . found where to
look."[9]

Indeed, when Augustine searches the locus of the self he discovers
a good many trinitarian likenesses. For example, in the experience of
knowing something there may, on the surface, seem two aspects to
knowledge: knower and thing known. But Augustine notes that if we
examine our own knowing activity more deeply, we will note a third,
namely, the knowledge itself which unites knower with known.[10]

Similarly, Augustine's theological depth psychology enables him to
call attention to other trinitarian psychic structures: memory, understanding, and the will that enables and binds together the other
two;[11] or, as has already been referred to in the introduction, there
is remembering, contemplating, and the love that as third empowers
memory and reflection in life.[12] And this is not the end of Augustine's
list of trinitarian lifelikenesses.[13]

But of his whole list, the greatest likeness of all is, for Augustine,
the experience of love. "By love," he writes, "the whole Trinity dwells
in us as in an inborn affinity."[14] So, in the four chapters that conclude
book 8 of Augustine's work, he dwells at length on the likeness of the
Trinity in the experience of love, concluding with these observations:

> Behold, then, there are three things: he that loves, and that which is loved, and love. What then is love, except a certain life which couples or seeks to couple together some two things, namely him that loves, and that which is loved? And this is so even in outward and carnal loves. But that we may drink in something more pure and clear, let us tread down the flesh and ascend to the mind. What does the mind love in a friend except the mind? There, then, also are three things: he that loves, and that which is loved, and love.[15]

This is the hinge. On it Augustine's argument turns, and a door opens to an understanding of the three-in-oneness which is the ultimate ground of all.

And why not? Has not the metaphor of love-and-marriage dominated the history of religions as a way of speaking about the unifying relationships among the gods, about the link between God and humankind, and about the connections within the aspects of the soul? Yet in the case of the household (*oikonomia*) of a god who is taken to be three, it would immediately seem, from Augustine's viewpoint, that the specifically Christian notion of love and marriage imagines them to be some sort of *ménage à trois*.

If this correspondence between divinity and love triangles seems farfetched, albeit appearing in the writings of one of the church's great theologians, the reader may want to have a look at the Book of Hosea. Or one may wish to note the frequency with which Yahweh's relationship to the Jewish people is expressed reciprocally as one of marital fidelity and/or infidelity (see, for example, the Book of Judges). Similarly, there is the frequent use of the same metaphor when Christian scripture and theology speak of the church as the bride of Christ, the relationship between this bride and bridegroom often being one of adultery.[16]

Just as Plato spoke of the necessity of the implicit if ghostly third between opposite cosmic elements at creation, and just as Aristotle spoke of the necessity of the third in logical comparisons of opposite terms (a *tertium comparationis*), it is apparently possible to imagine, as religious traditions have imagined, that in matters of an ultimate love or a loving ultimate there is *necessarily* a triangle.

No wonder the notion of the Trinity is offensive to the Church, which moves the divine image backward into binary theology and into dialogical religiosity, as the idea is also offensive in Jungian psychological quarters, which moves it forward to mandalas and quaternities. A threatening fantasy lurks in the trinitarian image: *the necessity of the third in love.*

Nonetheless the Church has said firmly that we may be saved if we stick with this fantasy and meditate upon it deeply in the self. The creed that is known as the *Symbolum quicumque* because of its opening words (*quicumque vult salvus esse*, whoever would be saved) says, "He, therefore, that would be saved let him think thus of the Trinity [*i.e.*, that the Trinity is a unity and that the unity is a Trinity]."[17] Further, the Church has said that we will be anathema if we do not face this three-as-oneness; that is, we will be damned if we failed to see the power of this three-in-one imagery.

Perhaps the insight is not so misplaced. After all, *literal* marriages begin in a triangle. The church's formula in the wedding liturgy does not marry two people. Rather, it speaks of "one man, one woman, and God." The third of this constellation, like that of the Holy Trinity itself, is a nonsubstantialistic factor, differing from the other two in kind, yet one with them in the wedding. And so it goes throughout the marriage, as if marriage were ineluctably a triangle. There is one man, one woman, and love. If this fails, then perhaps there will be one man, one woman, and a pet animal or a mutual hobby. Or there may come a time when she notes, not without appropriate jealousy, that he seems wed to his work, which is now a third in the marriage. And, of course, there are a seemingly infinite number of triangles when children come along. But the children grow up and leave home. So the wife seeks another third: gardening, jogging, country club, service club, an education she never finished, or a new life in business. In midlife there may come therapy as a third, or a lover for the man or woman or both. We enact the triangle dramatically and eternally. Nor does it ever end, for at the end there comes the angel of death, a crucial and ultimate third bringing to a focus the concerns and the cares, the anxieties and griefs, the unity and the differentiations of the love of one man and one woman, two who have dwelled together (*oikonomia*) as one.

It is an "affair" from beginning to end, a *ménage à trois*, a divine menagerie of love. The formula of the Christian doctrine of the Trinity, together with its residual fantasy, brings to expression what we all know all-too-well from life. Contemporary theologian Tom Driver, like that ancient one, Augustine, continues the sense when he writes:

In every relation of one to one, a third element is present. There is no way for one to relate to another without "something else" coming up, and this not as a mere distraction but as the necessary condition and consequence of the relation. Every dyad turns out to be a triad. We may dream of "a bicycle built for two," but then it turns out that we cannot get rid of the bicycle.

Then the author gives some examples:

A couple decide to hitch up, steal away, and live in a shack in the woods. The next thing they know, they are having to repair the shack.

Two lovers look raptly into each other's eyes. The next thing they know, they are talking about some movie they saw. If not that, they talk about the "love" they made an hour ago, or the food in the refrigerator, or the music on the radio, or the warmth of the bed they're in. They cannot remain in relation to each other if they do not refer to something "else."

Driver's other examples are not literally from the realm of love, but the Augustinian clue concerning the bonding which is experienced in love informs them nonetheless, as if love permeates experiences that may seem far from loving.

A prisoner stands before a judge. The two are locked in their roles. It is a charade unless they can both appeal to something "else," which is either expediency or justice.

And again:

A scientist observes certain data in the laboratory. She records the data. The information makes no sense unless it can be referred to something "else," which is called a theory.[18]

The likeness to life of the formula of the Trinity is compelling and clear, and the clue to the lifelikeness is love. Wallace Stevens wrote:

A man and a woman
Are one.
A man and a woman and a blackbird
Are one.[19]

Or, in the words of Novalis:

When numbers, figures, no more hold the key
To solve the living creature's mystery.
When those who kiss and sing have knowledge more
Than all the deeply learned scholars store,
. . . . . . . . . . . . . . . . . . . . . . . . . . . . . . . .

Then will a secret word oblige to face,
All of this made perversity.[20]

Perhaps the secret word is "Trinity."

The obvious compelling quality of the Augustinian argument concerning the lifelikeness between Divine life and human love makes all
the more surprising his further twist—another turn, so to speak, of
his hinge. The turn is apparently an about-face. Augustine no sooner
convinces himself and his reader about the likeness between a love
deeply understood and the Holy Trinity, than he turns around and
speaks strongly about their unlikeness. He says forthrightly that we
must not compare the image of threeness in the self to the Trinity
itself, but rather we must "discern in likeness, of whatever sort, a
great unlikeness, also."[21]

Augustine also writes, "Who can explain how great is the unlikeness, in this glass, in this enigma, in this likeness?[22] And, "We certainly seek a trinity—not any trinity, but that Trinity which is God,
the true and supreme and only God."[23] Toward the end of the book,
Augustine insists, "A thing itself, then, which is a trinity is different
from *the image of* a trinity in some other thing [*e.g.*, the self]."[24] The
likeness, it would seem, is a metaphor whose power is in its unlikeness
as much as in its likeness. So, Augustine reminds the reader, "The
apostle does not say, We see now a glass, but, We see now *through* a
glass."[25]

How are we to understand this paradox?—the self and its experience of love is like the Trinity which it is unlike. It is as if Augustine
is encouraging one to look for likenesses in things that are unlike each
other, and to look for the unlikenesses in things that seem to be similar. The saying sounds like a Zen koan: "Discern in likeness, of whatever sort, a great unlikeness, also."

However paradoxical this matter may seem, a similar insistence has
come recently from areas unlike theology: philosophy, literary criticism, and depth psychology. These additional testimonies can serve,
not as an understanding of the Augustinian theological paradox, but
as further amplifications of it.

*Identity and Difference.* The philosopher Martin Heidegger gave
a major lecture in June of 1957 on the principle of identity. In the
foreword to the published version of this lecture, there appears an

admonition to the reader that resonates with Augustine's paradox. Heidegger writes: "The close relation [*die Zusammengehörigkeit*, the belonging-together] of *identity and difference* will be shown in this publication to be that which gives us thought. The reader is to discover for himself in what way difference stems from the essence of identity."[26] Heidegger asserts at the outset that likeness and unlikeness belong together in profound philosophical thinking; therefore, the thinker will want to meditate on the way in which the separate and unique identities of things come about by virtue of their fundamental likeness.

In a time when "the center does not hold" (William Butler Yeats) and there is for many an "eclipse of God" (Martin Buber) and a "forgetfulness of Being" (Heidegger), the belonging-together of disparate aspects of life and meaning is problematic. In such a time, Heidegger suggests, identity and difference cannot come into an integrated relationship *as long as* one thinks of the identity of belonging-together as a belonging-*together* (*die ZUSAMMENgehörigkeit*), because this suggests, Hegelian fashion, "the unity of a manifold, combined systematically, mediated by a unifying center of authoritative synthesis."[27] But systematization, centering, and authoritative synthesis do not compel persons living in the fragments of a riddled world. According to Heidegger, there is another way to think the nature of identity and difference, namely, as *belonging*-together (*die ZusammenGEHÖRIGKEIT*), wherein the unity is determined by the belongingness, rather than the belongingness being determined by the unity.[28]

Heidegger characterizes this second way as "a leap" ("ein Sprung").[29] It is not a Kierkegaardian leap of faith nor a Hegelian leap into synthesis ("Aufhebung"). Rather, it is a springing into the abyss ("so in den Abgrund springt"), which entails a nose dive into the differentiations of life. In the variety of unlikenesses in life one may begin to sense a vibrant resonance ("der in sich schwingende Bereich"), wherein things which one may not have thought belong-*together* are nonetheless *belonging*-together.[30] If one could think one's experience and experience thinking in this way, then one would discover for oneself the close relationship of identity and difference. Such is the potentiality of a depth philosophy grounded in the *Abgrund* rather than in God or the one.

*Antimetaphor or Absolute Metaphor.* Something similar to the philosophical argument of Heidegger has lately occupied the theorizing of a variety of literary critics. Beda Allemann writes about "antimetaphor" or "absolute metaphor."[31] Stanley Hopper and Philip Wheelwright have spoken of "diaphor."[32] Jacques Derrida insists upon the centrality of the notion of "différance."[33] And an array of so-called deconstructionist critics, such as Harold Bloom, has pointed to the poetic figures which function, not by connecting, but by disconnecting—"like a wave breaking on a rock, giving up/Its shape in a gesture which expresses that shape."[34]

It had been assumed that the poetic seeing of likenesses between things which are unlike ("My love is like a red, red rose") is made possible by an implicit third, a *tertium comparationis*, which—like a Hegelian synthesis under the aegis of absolute spirit, or the belonging-*together* of all things under Kierkegaard's God or Plato's Being—makes all things cohere. When Homer says "Achilles is like a lion in battle," we imagine, or so the Aristotelian theory has it, that both man and animal share in bravado. But what happens to poetic meaning—in a play by Samuel Beckett or Harold Pinter, a novel by Julio Cortázar or Edmond Jabès, or a poem by Wallace Stevens or Ezra Pound—when we are deprived of the third, when the third has become a ghost? *Tertium non datur* (a third that is not given) can work as the connecting function in either logic or in metaphor. What then happens to a sense of meaning in a text?

The critics we have mentioned suggest that poetry can be of assistance. The artist is preeminently one who is at home in "achieving the negative" (Franz Kafka, *The Great Wall of China*) among the disparity of experiences and images. It was Julián Marías who, following the Spanish philosopher José Ortega y Gassett, observed that "in old Sanskrit poetry, most comparisons were introduced not by 'like' but by a negation."[35] So, Robert Burns's line would read "My love is *not* a red, red rose." The most deeply rooted likenesses—love, life, death, meaning—are unspeakable; a *via negativa* is required. It is as if to say, "I don't know the ultimate connection." The most radical metaphors make the connections, therefore, out of difference, out of what we do not know and cannot say, rather than out of what we think we know and about which we too often chatter.

*Gottähnlichkeit and Inflation.* It is just at this point that a curiosity in the writings of the psychologist C. G. Jung is relevant. In some of Jung's early writings (1912–1916) the term *Gottähnlichkeit* (god-likeness) appears prominently to designate a particular psychological situation. But not only does this term disappear in later writings, in later editions of the earlier works (after 1917) *Gottähnlichkeit* is replaced in the text by the term "inflation."[36]

Jung says that he borrowed the term *Gottähnlichkeit* from Alfred Adler.[37] Its particular function and meaning can best be described by the specific therapeutic situation it means to name.

Sometimes, during the course of her or his life, a person will identify unconsciously with a figure from past ego-history. She or he will adopt the persona of, perhaps, mother or father, teacher or therapist. At other times, the identification will be, not with some actual figure out of the past, but with an archetypal configuration. Then the person will act out Oedipus's jealousy, Christ's goodness, Hermes's boyish ulterior tricks, Hera's wrath, etc. In therapy, when such identifications are uncovered and the patient sees just who it is she or he is being like, a breakthrough occurs: "Not I, but Oedipus or mommy or daddy in me." It is a relief. One has discovered a god-likeness and now has a new insight into mood and behavior. Often a release from guilt, shame, or anxiety accompanies such a breakthrough.

But there is, as Jung discovered, a problem precisely in this therapeutic solution to personal problems. An inflation may attach to this new insight: "I am a god, an archetypal pattern, rather than little old me!" Like the sin of spiritual pride that often attaches to the grace of religious conversion, therapy can carry with it a false sense that "now I know something about myself." So, Jung counseled,

> The only person who escapes the grim law of *enantiodromia* is the one who knows how to separate himself from the unconscious.[38]

This suggests that the therapeutic goal is to discover the unlikeness of that which ego is like. Therefore, Jung added, the only person who escapes is

> the one who knows how to separate himself from the unconscious, not by repressing it — for then it simply attacks him from the rear — but by putting it clearly before him as *that which he is not.*[39]

Or, as Jung also said,

> The aim of individuation is nothing less than to divest the self of the false wrappings of the *persona* on the one hand, and of the suggestive power of primordial images on the other.[40]

As with Augustine, so with Jung!—I am not like the Trinity which I am really like!

Plotinus, a thinker with whose work Augustine was well acquainted, put the paradox in focus. In an essay, "Concerning Virtues," Plotinus observed that there are two sorts of "likeness" (*to homoiotai*). One is the likeness between things that are the same; the other is the likeness between things different.[41] A person could be virtuous, Plotinus argues, by being like moral men and women. Our own morality would then be an imitation of the likeness between like things. Plotinus thinks there is a deeper or higher virtue: "The serious matter is not to be without sin [which is achieved by being like virtuous people]: but rather the serious matter is to be like God [whom we are not like]."[42] Virtue consists, then, in leading back (*epistrophē*) the imaginal patterns within the self to the archetypal paradigms provided by the rich variety of forms found in the myths of divinity, of which the Trinity is, of course, one.[43]

The implication of Augustine's paradox concerning likeness and unlikeness suggests that there are two ways to go wrong in remembering the Trinity. One is to think dogmatically that the ultimate Trinity, the triune godhead, is *merely* unlike anything in life— "infinitely qualitatively distinct," "wholly other." The other mistake is to imagine pietistically that the Trinity is *merely* like the deep self—an "absolute immanence," *imitatio Christi*. Either way is a form of literalistic fundamentalism, and can lead to an inflation which may allow one to imagine that she or he is in possession of some ultimate religious truth. The prophets of Israel called this idolatry. The arrogance of one-sided understandings takes the offense and paradox out of religious meaning. It deprives life of mystery. As Augustine wrote in his work *On Free Will:* "To understand the Trinity soberly and piously occupies watchful care."[44]

Religion's images (Trinity included) do not refer in the first place, either negatively or positively, to behaviors. At least, such powerful images do not refer to behaviors of mortals as literalistically unlike or like them. Rather they bring to expression perspectives, attitudes, moods, intuitions, ways of seeing. It is not that marriage is the meaning of the Trinity; it is that the Trinity is the meaning of marriage. Augustine urges his reader not to think that the meaning of the

Trinity is found in actual marriages, but rather in "the hidden wedlock of man and woman within each self."[45] This is to say that marriage is not the only marriage one experiences in life. There are many marriages, and, in a trinitarian view, they are ultimately all triangles. There are many trinities, for trinity is a way of seeing all things, including actual literal behaviors.

As James Hillman said, "Behavior is fantasy, and fantasy is behavior, and always."[46] Our behaviors in ego's history are fantasies when they are occasions for seeing the way meaning is structured. Our actual loves can lead us to the trinitarian way of seeing. We do not see a glass; we see *through* a glass darkly. The likeness between the human experience of love and the ultimate unity of threeness is a likeness that is not like anything we can know. Such likeness leads into the abyss rather than out of it. It leads us to see that the life we thought we were leading is considerably more, something other. We are not what we are; and we are what we are not.

As Nicholas Berdyaev wrote:

> There does exist a commensurability between God and man, not man however as a natural and social creature. . . . The existential dialectic of the divine Trinity, as also the dialectic of the divine and the human, takes place in the very depths of existence.[47]

It is in the interest of preserving such depth that it becomes necessary to move from memory to contemplation, from remembering the fantasia of the trinitarian image and idea to the complex and variegated mythos that lurks below and within that which we are not, so that we may see what we finally are: the image of a myth.

PART TWO

# CONTEMPLATING
# IN THREES

# 3

## THE TRAGIC
## VISION OF THE TRINITY
### Trinitarian Contemplation
### in Ancient Myth

Probing the mythos that lurks behind and within the fantastical images of theology's later ideas is like exorcising the ghosts that haunt religious ideas. There are many ghosts, and not all of them are holy. Nor will they go away if ignored. In fact, one might better say that the work of mythic contemplation of the Trinity is not to exorcize but to exercise the depth of trinitarian meaning.

A polytheistic and archetypal perspective on the Christian monotheistic religion wants to discover what hides, perhaps well repressed and too often forgotten, in the logic of the theology. The task is not, however, accomplished by asserting allegorical typologies, farfetched correspondences, or clever free associations between theological ideas and ancient mythical themes; nor is it accomplished by historical and genetic tracing of the connections that may or may not exist in the so-called evolution of consciousness from Mediterranean mythology to Greek philosophy to Christian theology. The first work would be trivial, subjectivistic, and mere fancy; and the second, even were it possible, which is unlikely, would be irrelevant by virtue of its being merely intellectualistic.

The authentic work begins, not in sensation (history) or thinking (typology), but in feeling and intuition.[1] It calls for a sense of *mythoi* for the stories which bring to expression the deep complexities lying in the image of the love triangle that is key to the idea of the Trinity. If it is an exorcism of ghosts haunting theology's ideas, the exorcism may happen by exercising the myths which bring those ghosts to holy expression. And those ghosts are legion!

C. G. Jung was partial to the formula *Hermes ter unus* (Hermes, ree in one).[2] Erich Neumann drew attention to the trinity of ᵣᵣermes, Athena, and the mortal hero Perseus.[3] The Orphic tradition emphasized Zeus himself as a trinity, his head in the sky, his trunk on the earth, and his feet in the watery underworld, as if the cosmos is the triune body of god.[4] A Homeric hymn describes Dionysos's dismemberment by the Titans as specifically three pieces of the one god.[5] Hesiod focused on two triads of gods: Chaos, Gaia, and Eros at the beginning; and Ouranos, Kronos, and Zeus throughout all time.[6] James Ogilvy has written of still another mythos in trinity, saying, "We moderns would do well to reflect on the transformation of the Trinity of Zeus, Apollo, and Dionysos into their more recent mythological counterparts, the superego, ego, and id."[7] Norman O. Brown has written of Mars, Venus, and Harmonia.[8] Carl Kerényi has spoken in this vein about the three night goddesses, the *Nyktes*,[9] and he also wrote about the "many trinities of sisters" in Greek myth who seem to revolve in a "round dance,"[10] as he called it, around the figure of the moon goddess Niobe.[11] Kerényi also wrote about the divine triads of Zeus, Hera, and Apollo; Leto, Apollo, and Artemis; and of "Aphrodite's [*i.e.*, love's] situation in the midst of a male pair."[12] And need one mention Oedipus and Orestes, whose tragic triangles scarcely fail to haunt our lives, even when we forget their stories? We exercise what we fail to exorcize.

Nor do all these exhaust the possible pagan background *mythoi* of the Christian Trinity. A rigorous case has been built by Jung, Preisigke, and Jacobson which suggests that the Greek mythemes in the instance of the Christian Trinity were, if not irrelevant, at least derivative. The three-in-one notion, or so the argument goes, was passed from Egyptian mythology into Hellenistic syncretism, from which source Christian theologians took it. The Egyptian mythologem in question has to do with the hieroglyph of *ka*. *Ka-mutef* (the bull of the mother) is the procreative power that links father and son into a unity. For early Coptic Christians in Egypt, *ka* and Holy Ghost were the same.[13]

As intellectually interesting as this argument may be, it is not quite to the point of the present exploration. It is a historical argument finally. Even were it true — and how could anyone ever know for certain? — the question of meaning is begged. It is the question of the deep complexities of human sense that is at stake here. If we do not

wish to lose the insight about the Trinity from the experience of the
love affair — staying doggedly with the clue about eros in the godhead
from Augustine — then surely the myths that are the most crucial are
those that concern the marriage of Zeus and Hera, and the impossible
triangles which emerged in that context.

Zeus's affairs are well known. They are complained about by
philosophers, poets, and theologians — not to mention by Hera. For
example, Xenophanes objected, saying, "Homer and Hesiod have
attributed to the Gods everything that is a shame and reproach
among men, stealing and committing adultery and deceiving each
other." And Aristophanes uttered a comically sarcastic complaint: "If
you're caught in adultery . . . bring Zeus as your example for a
defense."[14] Everyone resists triangles and trinities, it seems, and for
good reason. They are extraordinary in number — at least in the case
of Zeus.

One remembers just a few of Zeus's secret liaisons when one says
the names of Dione, Maia, Leto, Demeter, Io, Persephone, Lethe,
Semele, Ganymede, Tyche, Nemesis, Leda, Europa, Eurynome, Aeginus, Dia, Alkmene, the Danae, and *all* the nymphs of the Titans.
Only Medea refused Zeus's advances . . . and we know what happened to her! The third in the marriage of Zeus and Hera is many,
as if the third can be anything, and is, in fact, everything. Everything
can be triangulated creatively with the gods, with the ultimate relationship, caught between Zeus and Hera, on the threshold of a divine
marriage (*hieros gamos*), in the rift between extremes, on the boundary of the "coincidence of oppositions" (*coincidentia oppositorum*).

In this mythic context it is not so difficult to see why the third is
necessary. Without it the pleroma would not be peopled. There
would be no gods and goddesses. We would have no myths, no
archetypal images of the soul's complex meanings. There would be
no variety for our individuations, for from these affairs, just the ones
that have been mentioned, there are produced Aphrodite, Hermes,
Apollo, Artemis, Dionysos, Zagreus, Helen, Asopus, Perseus,
Peirithous, and Herakles. The trinity is thin disguise to the truth of
polytheism in theology and in life, even in monotheistic theologies
and monotonous lives.[15]

The complexities are varied and subtle. Since no man or woman
sees god and lives, Zeus comes disguised in these stories, just as do our

life's triangles. God enters life's history as a bedraggled cuckoo, a
quail, a serpent, a bull, a cloud, a shower of gold, a stallion, and—
wonder of wonders—to one woman, god (*i.e.*, Zeus) comes as her
husband, which is to say, as a man. In fact, just as Yahweh makes a
bond of fidelity and love with the people of Israel, and just as God
comes to Christians in the form of a bridegroom, so Zeus's sexual
exploits are an expression of the way that divine and immortal reality
touches life and body and history and mortality. It is as if sensuality
in religious phenomenology is affirmed as one way of realizing or
becoming conscious of the deathless and ultimate truth about life.
God is made man, and of course he suffers.

Zeus suffers Hera, and she suffers, too. She becomes insufferably
jealous. Hera is right. She has been abandoned. "My God, my God,
why hast thou forsaken me?"[16] But at this moment emotion and feeling enter the marriage. The situation of the triangle has put Hera in
touch with herself and with her opposite. The broken dyad brings a
third, a bit of spirit, a shadow, a shade, and some soul, just as the
third brings brokenness. The situation of the triangle is a threshold,
a door to a new consciousness, a new way of seeing . . . trinitarianly.
As Jesus said to his disciples in a similar moment of suffering just
before the crucifixion, "If I do not go away, the Counselor [Com-
forter, Spirit, Holy Ghost] will not come to you."[17]

By following the ghostly mythos of the Trinity into its mythic backgrounds, the idea of the doctrine is deepened. The trinity in the context of the Zeus/Hera triangle presents a tragic view of life. (This may
be another way of saying what Jung may have meant when he
pointed to the Trinity as "incomplete.") But humankind needs images
of brokenness. And the Trinity implies not only that Spirit comes
cruciformed, in the crucifixions of crossed relationships, whether in
society or in the self, but also that in the soul's various broken connections there is Spirit, as long as one keeps the perspective of the triangle and attends to the third as ghost, the haunts of love. It is like
saying: the brokenness *is* the connection; the suffering, a loving!

It is the redemptively tragic dimension of the Trinity which has
been noted by Arthur McGill. In *Suffering—A Test of Theological
Method*, McGill takes a bold look at the problem of the Trinity.

> In the last two centuries the doctrine of the Trinity has been almost a
> dead letter for much Christian thought. Schleiermacher thought it in

need of revision [McGill might have also mentioned Karl Rahner, Jürgen Moltmann, and many others], and even so orthodox a figure as Karl Barth gives it a routine treatment in the first volume of his *Church Dogmatics.* At the popular level it is considered to be nothing but a feat of intellectual nonsense. God is supposed to be one and three at the same time. If you find this unintelligible, that simply proves how incomprehensible is the reality of God and how bold is the Christian faith! Needless to say, any doctrine that makes God into a numerical monstrosity and that treats his presence in Christ as serving to stupefy the human mind should be rejected out of hand.[18]

But McGill does not reject the Trinity. In the context of a book on the problem of suffering, he can speak in a new way about the meaningfulness of this doctrine.

"The problem is not," McGill writes, "how can the three persons of the Trinity, each genuinely distinct from the others, and each fully God, be conceived as one."[19] Indeed, for McGill, the problem is not philosophical or mathematical at all. Rather, the meaning of the problematic of an ultimate reality which is unified by being separated into the Father and the Son and the Ghost is captured in the phrase "needy, yet still God"! McGill's point is that "God's unity is a unity of love," as we have already noted in part 1 of this work. It is "a unity in which the identity of each party is not swallowed up and annihilated but established."[20] The idea of the Trinity suggests to McGill that "there must be a receptive, dependent, needy pole within the being of God."[21] This is to say that the Christian vision of ultimate reality gives expression to dependencies and sufferings in love which are, nonetheless, not weaknesses but strengths. "It is pride — and not love," McGill argues trinitarianly, "that fears dependence and that worships transcendence."[22] The Father needs the Son to carry on the work. The Son needs the Father in his failure. They are one in love, which is the Spirit of their relationship.

McGill sees important human meaning in a theology of the Trinity, and he is able to see it by looking at suffering — the suffering in love, and the love which is implied in the sense of suffering we feel. McGill depicts theologically what is already sensed dramatically in the stories of Zeus and Hera. This vision and its mythos are not easy. But then what is? The Trinity's vision is tragic — and redemptively so.

The doctrine of the Trinity can provide an important insight in life, but it is an insight that is easily missed when religion's theology becomes a prettified illusion (Freud) or an opiate (Marx). Theology shows the shadow-side, the ghosts that haunt. As Rilke said, "the gods cast shadows" ("von den Gottern ein Schatten fällt").[23]

But, precisely because the images of religions are so realistically complex, the doctrines of theology can be of assistance in helping people to bring life's pain to articulate expression. Theology gives us insight about our pain, just as our painful experiences provide a way of entering into the deeper meanings of our religious ideas.

James Hillman has observed something very similar in his work as a psychotherapist. He has noted how important the grotesque aspects of the stories of myth can be in sensing the meaning of everyday life.

> Mythology's moments of anxiety, bestiality, and possession, its extra-ordinary nonhuman imaginal happenings, can be newly illumined through our own corresponding experiences. Mythology can then reach us, and we it, in a fresh way because it bears directly on our pain. More: our pain becomes a way of gaining insight into mythology. We enter a myth and take part in it directly through our afflictions. The fantasies that emerge from our complexes become the gate into mythology. This way suggests a new method for the study of mythology, a method of fantasy.[24]

So it is with theology, too; but only if the theology is deepened, only if we can begin to remember the images of the ideas, and contemplate the shaded and nuanced *mythoi* in those images thus remembered. Then, theology is life; and life can be sensed as enacted theology.

This suggests that faith, were it to be really felt, could be felt deeply in pathology. (See the introduction, p. 6.) There is a therapeutic religious value, as well as a psychological value, in being faithful to the images of our deepest feelings and hurts. Our theology is discovered there. Surely it cannot be without significance that the church's intuition has been to link confession with faith, as if, were a person to articulate where life hurts, she or he will be able to see what is believed, not an ego believing, but the fantasies of the belief of self to which one has been faithful with a fidelity of deepest heart and mind, consciously or unconsciously. "Repent and believe," says the faith, as if these go together and belong together. Or, as Jung said, "Every experience of the self is a defeat for the ego."[25] The experience of deepening often hurts; hurts deepen.

Greek myth stays with triangular pain in the interest of trinitarian insight. Niobe's three faces are the three faces of lunacy. The Furies and their later counterparts, the three weird sisters, are our tragic fate. Oedipus and Orestes know that the triangles of life tell the *mythoi* of our sufferings. The Greeks had great difficulty keeping distinct the stories of the three Fates, the three Muses, and the three Graces. The triple goddess sideslipped easily for the people from one to the other, as if whatever is fated in life may be a grace if it were mused upon. Or as if what graces life in brilliance (Aglaia) and joy (Euphrosyne) and bloom (Thalia) will make a person weird or furious, but in the process produce, if not amusement, at least transpersonal images of the muses or poetizings of life. One may muse about the graces of the gods, but one's theologizings are never far from the fates of soul. The oldest of the triple goddesses knows this best. Her name is Hekate.

This uncanny Greek mythic figure combined the characteristics of moon (lunar sky), earth, and underworld. Such cosmic triplicity made possible her benefiting of mortals with riches and good luck. She was invisible to women and men, but dogs could see her pass, and some thought she was followed by a pack of ghostly hounds. The dog was witch-Hekate's sacred animal, and her witchcraft had especially to do with ghosts (those things which though thought to be dead, still "hound" or "dog" people). Hekate could be found at crossroads and the Romans named her Trivia. She was sometimes identified with Artemis (moon), Persephone (underworld), Demeter (earth), and Rhea (magic associated with death).

Hekate, not unlike the suffering servant of Isaiah, is despised and acquainted with grief. She embodies pain. Mythic tradition tells that she was purified in the river Acheron, whose name is derived from *achos*, meaning pain.[26] Being purified by pain, Hekate is, not surprisingly, often and in many ways identified by various triangulations.

She is caught between Artemis and Demeter. She also forms the underside of a triangle with Demeter and her daughter, Persephone.[27] In both *Orphic Hymn*[28] and Hesiod's *Theogony*,[29] Hekate is called *trioditin* (one goddess who is three). Like Zeus of the Orphic tradition, she is *ouranion* (sky), *chthonian* (earth), and *einalian* (sea). Three animals are attributed to her: either lion, dog, and mare, or lion, goat, and serpent. She is also associated with Kerberos, the three-headed dog. Though her name may mean "many-headed" (*hekaton* = hundred or many), her association with the three phases of the moon has earned her the epithet *trikephalos* (three-headed). She is also depicted as and called *triprosopos* (three-faced) and *triglena* (three-eyed). Nichomachus of Gerasa, in his mystical mathematical work *Theologumena arithmeticae*, takes advantage of the trinitarian mythos of Hekate to use her name for the number three. One is "monad" or same. Two is "dyad" or other. And three is the "mean between" or marriage to which Hekate belongs as third.[30]

Nor does Hekate's image fail to retain the sensual and erotic sense so important to trinitarian and triangular fantasy. Poseidonius underscores this by including Hekate as one of the orgiastic deities. In Thera the people remembered her along with Priapus whose ithyphallic nature is well known.[31] Kerényi wrote about Hekate: "Associations with a kind of eroticism that one may find crass and vulgar and a connection to souls and spirits are characteristic for her."[32] She is also called "thrice-whirled" (*trigladine*) as sexual affairs also so often are.

This is all to say that Hekate, well before Christianity, was carrying the trinitarian fantasy. But exploring her mythology enables us to see something more about the imagery than traditional theology typically allows.

As in the notion of the Christian Trinity, in the stories of Hekate the ghost is the factor that connects, that makes the triangle whirl. It creates the function of three heads, three modes of consciousness, rather than the oppositionalist perspective of two. The ghost gives a third eye. Hekate, like the Holy Spirit, is the lord of the ghosts, those who are purified by pain and whose function, precisely in being haunted by the experience of pain, is productive of a rampant love, linkings of eros born out of sympathy, empathy, and suffering.[33] This feeling for the lordship of the ghost makes Hekate consort of Hades in the Greek religious imagination. Her way of seeing is out of the deep.[34] She is even called *tartaropais* (child of the depths). And given her ability to go deep and to return from that realm, Hekate can be called *angelos* (angel) which means messenger and suggests thereby that she brings visions and dreams. According to the *Homeric Hymn*, she was the only one to bring "true news" to Demeter about Persephone's fate.[35] Hekate brings images, *phasmata polla* as they were called, helping one to imagine life when it is seen deeply.

What is implied in this Hekatean mythos is that imagination is located, in part, in the ghostings and hauntings within pain and sexuality, within the pain of sexuality, and within the eroticism of our pain. There we find our various sufferings to be thresholds because we get from these experiences images for our lives. Hekate is *prothyraia* (goddess of the threshold), by which two things are meant: a gate to the deeps of Hades's realm of soul, and the doorway to new life, for in this epithet Hekate is connected with Eleithyia, goddess of midwifery.[36] Images are born by and from ghosts. What haunts us and our relationships as the ghost of soul (*eidolon*) is an imaginal way for the images of psyche (*eidolon*).[37]

To celebrate the fact that a ghost is goddess of the boundary, the Greeks set up shrines where three roads met at the *tri via* (trivia), the crossing, the place where decisions must be made. And where decisions must be made is where one finds Hekate, that is, where one finds the god who is trinity.

The crux is that one may discover ultimate reality by way of triangulation, by way of life's crossroads, when one is on the boundary. Then a trinitarian mode of sensing life, beyond dualisms, dialectics, and either/or-ness, can emerge as a new threshold, a new doorway. Such a perspective has in fact been burgeoning of late, but not in theology.

Indeed, a Hekatean viewpoint gives clues concerning the prominence of the metaphor of boundary in much recent reflection in philosophy, letters, and science. It is as if trinitarian modes of understanding, in Hekatean guise, are resurfacing after several millennia of metaphysical and theological binitarianism, a failed either/or-ness of life's vision. We pause, therefore, to take note of some latter-day secular witness to the ghost of Hekate.

Interlude

# LIMINALITY, BOUNDARY, AND THE BETWEEN
## Trinitarian Contemplation in Contemporary Philosophy and Letters

Henry Corbin once argued that the traditional architecture of the temple was triadic, symbolically symmetrical to the celestial temple (intelligence, soul, and subtle body of the spheres) and to the structure of gnostic anthropology (spirit, soul, and body). But we have lost the triadic sensibility, he argued, and wrote, "The anthropological triad was destroyed at the Council of Constantinople in 869. All that was left was the dualism of soul and body, or of spirit and body, of thought and extension, and let us remember that this happened way before Descartes. . . . Man thus lost his soul just as the heavens had lost theirs."[1]

Corbin may be correct. If he is, it would give theological and philosophical basis in Occidental history to the either/or-ness of common Western perspective, the perspective which phenomenologists call "the natural attitude," and which they wish we would "bracket" (*epoché*). But if Corbin is right, an irony emerges in our time: the religious idea of trinitarian perspective, which is made problematic by the very theology that gave it birth, is rediscovered by secular science, which has no stake in its religious truth! Johannes Kepler, in the sixteenth century, may serve as the first demonstration, though by no means the last.

Kepler was, of course, a theologian first and a scientist last as Arthur Koestler takes care to point out in recounting the fascinating tale of "gravity and the Holy Ghost."[2] When he studied Protestant theology at the University of Tübingen, Kepler became attracted by Copernicus's notion of a heliocentric universe. Kepler himself acknowledged that his interest in this physical matter was really *meta*physical, writing,

I was encouraged in my daring inquiry by that beautiful analogy
between the stationary objects, namely, the sun, the fixed stars, and the
space between them, with God the Father, the Son, and the Holy
Ghost.[3]

And then he added, "I shall pursue this analogy in my future cos-
mographical work."[4]

Pursue it he did. Twenty-five years later, as Koestler reports, Kepler
repeated his theological-astronomical credo: "It is by no means per-
missible to treat this analogy as an empty comparison; it must be considered by its Platonic form and archetypal quality as one of the
primary causes."[5] So Kepler could write:

The sun in the middle of the *moving* stars, himself at rest and yet the
source of motion, carries the image of God and Father and Creator. He
distributes his motive force through a medium which contains the
moving bodies, even as the Father creates through the Holy Ghost.[6]

The "force" that is the medium of motion is, of course, gravity: the
Holy Ghost as gravity; gravity a ghost! As Koestler appropriately concludes, "Kepler's answer came *before* the question — it was the answer
that begot the question."[7] That is, the questions concerning the plan-
ets and their astronomy were generated in Kepler's mind by the
answer provided by his stubborn adherence to a trinitarian theological mode of understanding. There is indeed a "ghost in the machine"
of this science! . . . and it is still there, perhaps more than before.

In 1940, Gaston Bachelard, a French chemist, soon to become philosopher of imagination, published *La philosophie du non* (The philosophy of no). In this work he argued that new discoveries in
quantum physics required a new "logic" for proper understanding.
Bachelard said, "The plunge has to be taken: one has to enter fully
into a new trinary system. . . . A new logical value needs to be
introduced in addition to the value *true* and the value *false*."[8] Following from the physics of Werner Heisenberg, the mathematics of
Erwin Schrodinger, and the philosophy of science of Henri Fevrier,
Bachelard spoke of a "three-valued logic."[9] He claimed that this
would entail "a new pedagogy"[10] by which persons could "free themselves from certain habits of thinking."[11] It would mean, Bachelard
observed before the more recent popularity of "deconstructionism,"
"a systematic education in deformation."[12]

Thirty-nine years after Bachelard penned these ideas, Gary Zukav popularized them in his widely read treatment of "the new physics" entitled *The Dancing Wu Li Masters.* The trinitarian way of thinking became necessary, Zukav explained, when physics was confronted with having to affirm that light and energy were both waves and particles, each at the same time.

> For most of us, life is seldom black and white. The wave-particle duality marked the end of the "Either-Or" way of looking at the world. Physicists no longer could accept the proposition that light is *either* a particle *or* a wave because they had "proved" to themselves that it was *both*, depending on how they looked at it.[13]

As Heisenberg had written, "It introduced something standing in the middle between the idea of an event and the actual event, a strange kind of physical reality just in the middle between possibility and reality."[14]

Zukav went on to show that the new physics also implied a third between other commonplace dualisms, such as that between something and nothing,[15] or between the perspectives of materialism and idealism.[16] As John Von Neumann had said, the logical calculus now required is "in contrast to the concepts of ordinary logic."[17] So David Finkelstein could write:

> There are no waves in the game. The equation that the game obeys is a wave equation, but there are no waves running around. This is one of the mountains of quantum mechanics. There are no particles running around either. What's running around are quanta, the third alternative.[18]

Zukav explains this mode of thinking with an anecdote: "During the Lebanese civil war . . . a visiting American was stopped by a group of masked gunmen. One wrong word could cost him his life. 'Are you Christian or Moslem?' they asked. 'I am a *tourist!*' he cried."[19]

With Zukav's tourist and with Finkelstein's quanta which are *not* the waves whose equations they obey and *not* the particles whose equations they equally obey, we are near to Kepler's Trinity and the Ghost. Indeed, when Einstein became aware of the fact that his photon theory contradicted Young's wave theory *without disproving it,* he speculated, as Zukav reports, "that photons were guided by 'ghost waves.' "[20] Surely science has become as radical as theology is supposed to have been.

Neils Bohr once remarked that "those who are not shocked when they first come across quantum theory cannot possibly have understood it."[21] Such wonder as men and women now feel in the face of the discoveries of science is not inappropriate to feel, and to the same degree, in the face of the Trinity of theology . . . especially since the structure of the insights, now as then, is so similar, if not identical.

*Neti . . . neti,* "neither this nor that": ultimate reality, or ultimately reality, is in the middle, but in a "middle" which is not a "thing" (ghost, *tertium non datur*).

While twentieth-century scientists were probing the archaeology of this middle, twentieth-century existentialist philosophers and theologians were discovering the same conceptual "between." Jean-Paul Sartre and Karl Jaspers, Martin Heidegger and Paul Tillich, not to mention Martin Buber, wrote of the "boundary" between finite and infinite, between Being and beings, whose topography marked the human condition at its most profound depths.[22] That the concern of these thinkers perdures is indicated recently (to give only two examples) in the writing of Charles E. Scott, *Boundaries in Mind,*[23] and Charles E. Winquist, "Body, Text, and Imagination." The latter notes, in a deconstructionist essay reminiscent of Bachelard's *Philosophy of No* and its "deformation," that "the theology of the future is a theology of a third order."[24]

Winquist traces his term "third-order theology" to the work of Gordon Kaufman.[25] It is precisely a debate between Kaufman and Paul Van Buren which allows purchase on a postmodern philosophical understanding of trinitarian thinking.

*Philosophy.* In 1966, Gordon Kaufman wrote a seminal essay in which he inquired as to the *actual* function of the concept of "God" in man's use of "God"-language.[26] He noted that most often and most notably the term for ultimacy occurs "within the context of man's sense of limitation," when there is a sense of what traditionally has been called "finitude." Therefore, as Kaufman says, "the idea of God functions as a *limiting concept,* that is, a concept that . . . refers to that which we do *not* know but which is the ultimate limit of all our experiences." "God-talk," as he calls it, "arises because certain features of experience force us up against the limit(s) of all possible knowledge and experience."[27]

In his analysis Kaufman posits four types of "limit": those of the physical-material environment; those of the organic body; boundaries imposed upon people by personal and external social factors; and certain normative limits, such as the limiting nature of the idea of true over against false or beautiful over against ugly, with no third possibilities.

On the basis of this differentiation of types of limits, Kaufman reasons that the personal God of Christian theism is a "limit"-concept analogous to the third type, the personal limits we sense from others in society. Man, Kaufman thinks, makes an analogy from this experience in everyday life to some sense of an ultimate limit. "When a personal limiter is the analogical basis for understanding the ultimate Limit," Kaufman reasons, "a doctrine of God results."[28] The most common Christian metaphors for the ultimate Limit help to make the point: Father, Lord, Judge, King, etc. For Kaufman these are indicators that the Christian limit-concept of God is grounded in the everyday experience of personal-social-historical boundedness.

Kaufman is really arguing *against* attempting to ground a doctrine of God philosophically in the language of metaphysical and cosmological dualism. Over against this he is petitioning for a language that is analogical.[29]

But Kaufman's argument found a limit of a different sort in the form of a response published in 1968 by Paul Van Buren.[30] Van Buren joined the issue directly, saying, "A sense of limitation is too narrow a definition of the experiential rootage of the language about the gods, even for Christianity." He argued that while many men and women through history may well have experienced limits of various sorts, nonetheless it is few indeed who have "trembled in the presence of the gods."

It is the experience of the "few" which interested Van Buren. For deeply religious men and women, he believes, it is not so much a sense of limit as it is a sense of "wonder" that calls forth talk about "God." To sense the limits of life is to view "the ordinary as ordinary," whereas in Van Buren's view the religious sensibility occurs when there is a seeing of "the ordinary as extraordinary."[31]

In this essay Van Buren was attempting to call attention to the fact that "every seeing is seeing as," and so he emphasized "imaginative vision," parabolic utterance, dreams, and poetry as typical of the logical models for philosophy of religion.[32]

It is as if Kaufman had picked up one side of Rudolf Otto's definition of religion as *mysterium tremendum et fascinosum* (a fascinating and fearful mystery), and Van Buren had acknowledged the other side. Kaufman sees the *tremendum* of the experience of limit; Van Buren sees the *fascinosum* of wonder. Yet in this debate between notions of many and few, limit and wonder, *tremendum* and *fascinosum*, there was to come a third possibility.

Four years after he responded to Kaufman, Van Buren published a new book in which he addressed the problem of limit in a different way.[33] "Language has limits," Van Buren acknowledged. But the word "limit" may itself be misleading when speaking of these limits. This term, Van Buren observed, presents us with a "picture of a line that marks off one area within the limit from another area beyond, one which we can see just as well." A different image may be more useful, that of a squash court in which, unlike a tennis court with its clearly marked lines, "there is no 'out,' no possibility of marking the fall of the ball beyond the boundaries of the court."[34] So it is, also, Van Buren thinks, with language.

Language is like a platform. We can walk on it or dance on it, but if we go beyond the edge we simply fall off into non-sense. "Edge" is the word Van Buren uses to replace "limit" over which he and Kaufman had argued.[35] He calls his book *The Edges of Language*.

Some prefer to stay away from the edge. They like to have things clear. They are limited in imagination. And they have no sense of humor. But others make their home at the edges. Van Buren lists four instances of language lived at the edge: the language of jokes and puns, the language of lovers, the language of metaphysics, and the language of religion. Examples of these follow.

1. the language of jokes and puns—"A door is not a door when it is ajar!"
2. the language of lovers—"Even though all the stones of Baalbek split into exact quarters, and the rooks of Repton utter dire prophecies in Greek . . . I will love you whatever happens, even though you put on twenty pounds and become afflicted with a moustache!"[36]
3. the language of metaphysics—"In the labyrinth of metaphysics are the same whispers as one hears when climbing Kafka's staircases to the tribunal which is always one floor further up."[37]
4. the language of religion—"God is One and Three!"

Van Buren also mentions the parables of Jesus and the koans of Zen.[38]

Though Van Buren, as a linguistic philosopher of religion, feels "uneasy with the stumbling gait of walking language's frontier," he also wants "to use something more than the vague word 'mystery,' " as he had in his earlier essay.[39] Now, armed with the word "edge," and with examples of language's edges taken from human experiences, Van Buren can describe language about God as language "speaking at its edge." It would be a mistake, he believes, "to think that the word 'God' either falls well within the edges of language, where religious claims about God would be meaningful but would appear to be false, or else lies outside language altogether. Planted in its own ground, however, right on . . . the boundary of language, the word can be as alive and flourishing today as in the past."[40]

This boundary is no place for literalism, whether theistic or atheistic. Literalists, Van Buren writes, have the matter backward. It is not that things said about God (*i.e.*, that he is a father or good or loving or mighty) are to be seen as attributes which are qualities belonging to an object. Rather, these things are subjects about which one wants to say more than ordinary linguistic conventions will allow.

For example, when someone wants to say more about love than language permits, he can say, "God is Love," meaning that he has said all he can and that his language is on the edge. Though he cannot say any more in some literalist sense, he nonetheless does not wish to remain silent. Van Buren quotes T. S. Eliot:

> Words strain,
> Crack and sometimes break, under the burden
> Under the tension, slip slide, perish,
> Decay with imprecision, will not stay in place,
> Will not stay still. . . .[41]

Between literal and metaphoric, between *fascinosum* (identity) and *tremendum* (difference), there is a threshold which is the edge of language. On this "edge" is the philosophical "logic" of language about ultimate reality, and not only for philosophers of religion.

*Anthropology.* What Van Buren refers to as edge, Victor Turner, borrowing a term from a famous study on rites of passage by Arnold van Gennep, calls *limen.*[42] The word is Latin for threshold, and Turner, like Gennep before him, uses it to refer to the middle period in rituals of initiation, that most sacred moment of the ritual which

comes after the individual's separation from the social structure and
prior to his or her reintegration into the community. It is that time
which is characterized by a "transient humility,"[43] a condition that
Turner likens to Martin Buber's concept of *das Zwischenmenschliche.*

Buber writes of his notion in a manner particularly trinitarian! "In
the most powerful moments of dialogic, where in truth 'deep calls
unto deep,' it becomes unmistakably clear that it is not the wand of
the individual or of the social, but of a third which draws the circle
round the happening. On the far side of the subjective, on this side
of the objective, on the narrow ridge, where I and Thou meet, there
is the realm of the between."[44]

Not only does Turner analyze the liminality of persons in sacred
rituals, as, for example, in the Ashanti of Ghana, the Nuer of the
Sudan, and the Ndembu of Zambia, but he also extends the analysis
into social anthropology so as to identify other instances of "liminal
personae" or "threshold people," those who sense their lives as
"betwixt and between."[45] Examples are taken from Third World
nations, court jesters, monastics, millenarists, and bohemians, to
name only a few. In fact, to some degree the quality of liminality
could be seen as a characteristic generally of *religious* men and
women. So Turner writes: "What appears to have happened is that
with the increasing specialization of society and culture, with
progressive complexity in the social division of labor, what was in
tribal society principally a set of transitional qualities 'betwixt and
between' defined states of culture and society has become itself an
institutionalized state. . . . Transition has here become a permanent
condition."[46]

But as in the case of rites of passage, the condition of permanent
liminality may have an important function. Turner notes, "We are
provoked by silence, negativity, liminality, ambiguity, into efforts of
extended comprehension."[47] It is as if to say that somewhere between
what we may have sensed to be on the one hand a limit and on the
other hand a limitlessness or wonder, there is an edge. And if we
could live on this continuous threshold, life might itself take on an
edge, so to speak, and our comprehension might be considerably
extended beyond preconceptions about the limits of life and its limitlessness, extended perhaps in the direction of a "transient humility."

This may be the threshold spoken about by Wendy Doniger O'Flaherty, who has done for myth what Turner did for ritual. In an essay entitled "Inside and Outside the Mouth of God: The Boundary between Myth and Reality," O'Flaherty speaks of "the liminal jaws," the "permeable wall," and "the artificial barrier we impose between myth and reality."[48] She shows, with examples taken in the main from South Asian religion, that "myth sets out explicitly to dramatize the fact that the boundary between myth and reality is highly mobile."[49]

"Limit," O'Flaherty notes, may indeed "be construed as a barrier." But it may also be sensed as a border or as "a boundary line where fantasy and reality meet." It is on behalf of this second sense that O'Flaherty surveys myths of the mouth of God.

> One day when the children were playing, they reported to Yashodha, the mother of Krishna (who was an incarnation of the god Vishnu), "Krishna has eaten dirt!" Yashodha took Krishna by the hand and scolded him and said, "You naughty boy, why have you eaten dirt?" "I haven't," said Krishna. "All the boys are lying. If you believe them instead of me, look at my mouth yourself." "Then, open up," she said to the god, who had in sport taken the form of a human child. And he opened his mouth.
> Then she saw in his mouth the whole universe, with the far corners of the sky, and the wind, and lightning, and the orb of the earth with its mountains and oceans, and the moon and stars, and space itself; and she saw her own village and herself. . . . When she had come to understand true reality in this way, God spread his magic illusion in the form of maternal love. Instantly Yashodha lost her memory of what had occurred. She took her son on her lap and was as she had been before, but her heart was flooded with even greater love for God, whom she regarded as her son.[50]

It is as if our world is the dirt in God's mouth. Or perhaps it is that our dirt is the universe of God's mouthings. O'Flaherty urges us not to decide either for the one or the other. Rather, "the point of enlightenment," she says, is not being in the mouth or being out of the mouth, but being in transition, "the motion across the threshold."[51] One of mythology's functions is to keep life in this transition, not knowing, not literal, *neti . . . neti*, neither this nor that, to keep it moving, on the edge . . . liminal.

Turner and O'Flaherty are not alone among anthropologists in this trinitarian way of thinking. Jonathan Z. Smith has called attention to this triadic "logic" in the work of Evans-Pritchard. The particular instance is Neur religious consciousness wherein the people refer to twins as birds. Yet, they know that human infants are *not* birds. So "the formula," Evans-Pritchard writes, "does not express a dyadic relationship between twins and birds, but a triadic relationship between twins, birds, and God."[52]

Claude Lévi-Strauss investigates a similar trinitarian anthropologic in his essay "The Structural Study of Myth." When raising the question about "the basic logical processes which are at the root of mythical thought," he discovers a mode similar to that described by O'Flaherty and Evans-Pritchard. Lévi-Strauss writes: "Two opposite terms with no intermediary [like life and death] always tend to be replaced by two equivalent terms which admit of a third one as mediator [like agriculture and warfare with hunting in between]; then one of the polar terms and the mediator become replaced by a new triad [as for example, herbivorous animals, carrion-eating animals, and beasts of prey, all between agriculture and hunting]."[53] Lévi-Strauss concludes that the logic of myth has as its purpose overcoming contradictions in life by introducing three-dimensional models from myth.[54]

*Letters.* If myth may be viewed as functioning trinitarianly, so may poetry. This may be why contemporary literary critics, not unlike philosophers and anthropologists, have focused their attention on the motif of boundaries. For example, J. Hillis Miller has suggested that the anthropologists' word "liminal" describes with precision the experience a reader has, whether she or he knows it or not, when confronting the text of a poem.[55] Miller analyzes Shelley's *Epipsychidion* in order to demonstrate this point, but he means his demonstration to be but one example of the experience of creative literature in general.

As readers of a text we are like guests with a host, Miller notes. But when truly engaged in the experience of interpretation, as everyone always is, wittingly or unwittingly, it is impossible to know precisely which is guest and which is host. In the case of thoroughgoing engagement, we are "always [in] this in between zone," Miller writes, "neither inside nor outside."[56] We enter a "border zone" when encountering a piece of literature, often without noticing it. "This encounter may be compared," Miller says, "to the uncanny experience of reaching a frontier where there is no visible barrier, as when

Wordsworth found he had crossed the Alps without knowing he was doing so."[57] The poem, therefore, performs a sort of "deconstruction" of ego-certainty with regard to questions of meaning.

Harold Bloom has used the phrase "the breaking of form" to name this liminal poetic experience of deconstruction, whereby the radical experience of literature places ego on a threshold. Bloom suggests that the reader may wish to attend in poetry as in life to those radical moments of "topological displacement" which he calls "crossings."[58] This *topos* of the meaning of a poem is found in its trope, its turning figure, as in the example Bloom gives from a poem by John Ashbery.

> They seemed strange because we couldn't actually see them.
> And we realize this only at a point where they lapse
> Like a wave breaking on a rock, giving up
> Its shape in a gesture which expresses that shape.[59]

This focus on the liminal moment is like that crucial gap in a dream which James Hillman has referred to with the word "hiatus."[60] It is also expressed in one of Rilke's sonnets, in which the poet says "transformation . . . loves in the swing of the figure nothing so much as the point of turning."[61]

The deconstructive point concerning the *between* has been carefully charted, together with an iconoclastic warning, by Justus George Lawler in his book, *Celestial Pantomime*. He is concerned to take proper note of the radicality of metaphor—what Wheelwright called "diaphor"—in which the crucial third, Aristotle's *tertium comparationis*, is not given (*tertium non datur*), or, perhaps, is given in function by its absence in substantialistic fact. "This is the domain"— Lawler is speaking about poetic meaning—"where one leaps the gap between premise and conclusion without the 'middle term,' without having the joke 'spelled out.' "[62] The direction is from the triadic form of, for instance, romanticism (beauty-is-truth) to a dyad (truth-beauty) which functions as a unity. Lawler calls it "leaping the gap," where the function of the gap (the third which is not given) is a leaping (the imaginal third or ghostly imagination).[63] Lawler's warning comes when he is interpreting the poetry of John Donne. He alerts his reader against "heavy-handed explication" by interpreters "for whom the mention of 'three' sets off triadic tics—more lately replicated in the quest for the historical Trinity" in Donne's poetry.[64] The iconoclasm of Lawler's warning serves, of course, to deconstruct a literalist notion of the Trinity which has no proper understanding of the third term: ghost! The "hiatus" or "gap" or "void" becomes opaque; one is no longer on edge, not liminal.

William Spanos, editor of the important American literary journal *boundary 2*, has argued strenuously for an acceptance of the threshold-sense of edge as fundamental to contemporary experience and literature. In the initial volume of *boundary 2* (1972), Spanos described the postmodern literary imagination as functioning under the metaphor of boundary in the way that the premodern imagination had operated both explicitly and implicitly under the figure of the "detective."[65]

The modern imagination of the symbolists (*e.g.*, Stéphane Mallarmé, Marcel Proust, W. B. Yeats, Ezra Pound, T. S. Eliot, and James Joyce) shares with the postmodern imagination (*e.g.*, that of Samuel Beckett, Jean-Paul Sartre, Eugene Ionesco, Jean Genet, Harold Pinter, Thomas Pynchon, and Franz Kafka) a rejection of the perspectives of Aristotelian logic of narrative, that a well-made plot proceeds from a beginning through a middle to an end. They also are joined in rejecting the perspectives of a Western positivistic humanism, including the belief that man's vocation is one of utility in manipulating and controlling nature and self.

Paradigmatic for this double perspective of "the straightforward Western man of action" is the detective story in whose form there is implied a "monolithic certainty that immediate psychic or historical experience is part of a comforting, even exciting and suspenseful well-made cosmic drama or novel."[66] Spanos explains this in these words: "Just as the form of the detective story has its source in the comforting certainty that an acute 'eye,' private or otherwise, can solve the crime with resounding finality by inferring causal relationships between clues which point to it (they are 'leads,' suggesting the primacy of rigid linear narrative sequence), so the 'form' of the well-made positivistic universe is grounded in the equally comforting certainty that the scientist . . . can solve the immediate problem by the inductive method, a process involving the inference of relationships between discontinuous 'facts' that point to or lead straight to an explanation of the 'mystery,' the 'crime' of contingent existence."[67]

Though both modernism, in symbolist and other forms, and postmodernism are together in rejecting Aristotelian and humanist assumptions, they differ in their manner of rejection.[68] Spanos notes that "the affirmative formal strategy of Symbolist modernism was one of religio-aesthetic withdrawal from existential time into the eternal simultaneity of essential art."[69] This is not the way, however, of the literature and experience of postmodernism. Where Miller and Bloom used the term deconstruction to describe the radically poetic work, Spanos sees in the postmodern imagination what he calls an "aesthetic of decomposition" or *dépaysment*.

Thus it is no "accident that the paradigmatic archetype of the post-modern literary imagination is the anti-detective story . . . [which] evokes the impulse to 'detect' . . . in order violently to frustrate by refusing to solve the crime." If an author introduces some "sort of impassioned amateur detective," this postmodern antiheroic charac-ter "doesn't find anything." Far from purging the reader of his "fear and pity" (Aristotle), there is a generating of dread which has no object of a substantialistic nature, neither a physical nor yet a spiritual object.

Yet the function of postmodernist literature, Spanos believes, is not negative. Because it opens realms of meaning by distracting the ego's certainties away from monolithic understanding, such a poetic ulti-mately points toward "a literature of generosity" that is born of the "humility of acknowledged uncertainty" and a "willingness to let Being be." This may be important to us, and deeply so, because, as Spanos writes, "only in the precincts of our last evasions, where 'dread strikes us dumb,' only in this realm of dreadful uncertainty, are we likely to discover the ontological and aesthetic possibility of generosity." Thus, the postmodern imagination, being disenchanted with detective heroisms of a humanist and Aristotelian kind, brings to expression on our behalf an "on-going boundary situation."[70]

But Miller and Bloom seem to have implied something more than Spanos has. They all agree that boundary is a root metaphor of our time. Yet in Miller and Bloom there is implicit that the experience of metaphor, of living "poetically upon the earth" (Hölderlin), is not a matter of a particular historical epoch such as postmodernism, but is rather a matter of viewing life as eternally on a crossing, on the turn of a trope or two, on a border that is everywhere and always between two zones, gaps that are nowhere and never (not being literal "wheres" or "whens" at all).[71] Not only is boundary seen as metaphor, but metaphoric living is sensed as boundary-experiencing. This implicit turn in Bloom and Miller becomes explicit in the writings of another critic, Stanley R. Hopper.

By 1965, Hopper had spoken of "symbolic reality" as "things in their appearing doing so within boundaries."[72] But he testified that as long as man does not realize that his living is poetic, meandering through metaphors, he mistakes the nature of his boundaries and aims unconsciously to secure his ego through literal identifications.[73] Quoting Wittgenstein, Hopper wrote, "A picture holds us captive, and we cannot get outside of it, for it lay in our language, and language seemed to repeat it to us inexorably."[74] That is, we cannot get outside the limits of our language's imaginal perspectives because we take them literally.

Hopper had observed that the poet may be of help in this, because the poet is typically the one who treats language, and the boundary-experience with it, non-literally. Seeing metaphorically "implies a certain transparency," Hopper argued, "both within ourselves and toward all things."[75] So, radical metaphoric seeing enables us to have a sense of boundary as a moving back and forth across a threshold, a seeing through all things and through ourselves as well (meta-phor as dia-phor, diaphanous, like a veil through which all reality is unveiled precisely in its sensuous indirection).[76]

In 1972, Hopper continued to use the metaphor of boundary as a metaphor of the notion of metaphor itself. The title of his essay was a clue to its content: "Jerusalem's Wall and Other Perimeters."[77] "Our arts today," Hopper observed, "seem to be pointing to the necessity of unlearning those formulae and patterns which have walled us in." Then he changed the figure, moving in the direction of the Orient, saying, "We must empty the cup again." Formerly the "walls" of our ideas may have been "gates," as in Blake's poem: "It will lead you in at Heaven's gate,/Built in Jerusalem's wall."[78] But now, Hopper wrote, "Our concern lies at quite a different point. Kafka's 'Castle' . . . is a more realistic and durable myth at this moment in our history than 'Jerusalem's walls.' "[79]

In a more recent essay Hopper focused the boundary-experience within the image of the emptied cup, and in doing so he argued for the experience and the perspective as belonging to all ages. The cup emptied of so-called ego becomes the figure not only of the experience of the boundary but also of the experience of the non-literal. That is, it is not only the metaphor for boundary but it is also the boundary for metaphor.

In this essay, "The Bucket As It Is," Hopper mentions the limit-situation of life explicitly and in numerous forms. He speaks, for example, of the "between" and of the "rift" in the writings of Heidegger; the "boundary" of Jaspers; the "collision" of Kierkegaard; the "wall" of Nicholas of Cusa; and the "barrier" of the Zen-text of the *Mumonkan*. To these borders Hopper brings the poem itself, that is, the experience of things as metaphor where suddenly the cup or bucket of ego is emptied. The bottom drops out. Where before one had been "cut off from the depths" of experience, now, for a moment perhaps, one sees that one is seeing everything *through* that which had been thought formerly to *be* everything. "Is" becomes "as." Things move. They are no-things. Yet they are *like* other things.

All is threshold. As Theodore Roethke says in *In a Dark Time*, "edge is what I have." And just this experience gives an edge to life. It gives metaphor and metaphoric seeing. Whatever image comes at the boundary (for there is precisely where images pour in upon us) becomes itself a boundless source of meaning.

Hopper writes, "Here the between would seem to be the boundary between the ego and the deep self. It would appear . . . that it is by way of the deep self that being comes to presence,"[80] as if self were the threshold through which move the metaphors of reality, or as if metaphoric seeing were the threshold by which self becomes diaphanous to itself, a ghost, not unlike Hekate. The trinitarian implications of this Hekatean ghost, especially in relation to the concept of boundary, will be explored in the next chapter.

# 4

## ANGEL
## FACE AND BODY
### Trinitarian Contemplation in Neoplatonic, Gnostic, and Alchemical Theologies

To discover the mythological ghost of Hekate in the Christian theological idea of the Trinity (chap. 3), and then to note latter-day secular witnesses to this ghost of Hekate in philosophy, the social sciences, and literary criticism (the previous interlude) is to affirm the importance of the "third" factor in oppositional thinking, without imagining it to be some actual third thing. The third is a ghost, and it dwells on the threshold, at the boundary, so that it functions as a doorway. To focus on the ghost as a "thing" would be to lose the relationship between the two. "Two's company, three's a crowd!" But to deny the ghost, the one that haunts the life of loving connectedness between the two, is to locate the source of the spirit and love that unites in the two themselves, and the spontaneity and grace of the relation becomes a burden which cannot be borne. Father and son are not father-and-son, but merely two "infinitely qualitatively distinct" individuals, unless they are possessed by the spirit which binds in love.

Theologically viewed, Hekate's ghost warns against two misunderstandings. On the one hand, it would be a failure of spirit and an insistence on reason and will to neglect the third binitarianly. This is what has so often happened in Western Christendom, with its overemphasis on God the Father and on Jesus, the Christ, who is the Son, and its lack of emphasis on the Spirit and eros (see the introduction). But, on the other hand, Hekate's ghost warns against the literalist attempt to overcompensate for this failure. Spiritualist movements such as Pentecostalism or speaking in tongues note the lack in the orthodox church, but they attempt to correct it by reifying and sub-

stantializing the Spirit, making the third which is a ghost into some
actual thing, a thing of belief or a thing of pietistic experience and
practice. In the metaphor of marriage, this second faux pas would be
like accepting the fact that the two persons are united by a third
factor, say a mutual interest or the children or money, and then,
seeing the importance of the third to the relationship, worshipping
and adoring and loving that third, thereby forgetting that the love is
*between* the two.

But Hekate's ghost has not been altogether forgotten in Western
theology, even if she has haunted only the edges of theological thinking, and even if those edges have been in the main eliminated from
Christian teaching and practice. The mythological insight concerning the notion of the Trinity has been carried by Neoplatonism,
Gnosticism, and alchemy, all of these being pagan heresies that have
both haunted orthodoxy and been repressed by it, but whose perspectives may be crucial in our time if the Trinity is to be understood. The
trinitarian perspectives of these three — Neoplatonism, Gnosticism,
and alchemy — are all "footnotes to Plato" (Alfred North Whitehead).

Not only did Plato give the trinitarian formula in *The Republic* —
"Join the three in one"— but earlier, in *The Philebus*, he had reported
on Socrates's attempt to teach Protarchus the Hekatean perspective
on this formula. Part of the conversation follows:

> *Socrates.* Well, there are the three things I have spoken of, if you
> follow me.
> *Protarchus.* Yes, I think I see what you mean. You are asserting, I
> gather, two factors in things — first the unlimited, second the limit [like
> the unlimited God, the Father, and the limited historical Jesus, the Son,
> the incarnate one]. But I can't altogether grasp what you mean by the
> third thing that you mention [like the Holy Ghost?].
> *Socrates.* The reason for that, my dear good sir, is that you are con-
> fused by the multiplicity of that third kind [like the Spirit in every per-
> son's spirit?]. And yet a plurality of forms was presented by the
> unlimited too, and in spite of that we stamped on them the distinguish-
> ing mark of "the more" and its opposite, and so saw them as a unity.
> *Protarchus.* True.
> *Socrates.* Then again we did not complain about the limit, either
> that it exhibited a plurality, or that it was not a real unity.
> *Protarchus.* No, there was no reason to do so.
> *Socrates.* None whatever. And now as to the third kind, I am reckon-
> ing all this progeny of our two factors as a unity, and you may take me

to mean a coming-into-being, resulting from those measures that are achieved with the aid of the limit.[2]

Protarchus's difficulty, not unlike that of Western Christendom, is that he has difficulty conceiving of the third without thinking of it as a "thing" like the other two. And if it is not such a thing, then how can it be anything? But Socrates had already taught that in matters of ultimate Being it is not a matter of binitarianism nor of tritheism. As Plato wrote in the *Timaeus:* "It is not possible to combine two things properly without a third to act as a bond to hold them together."[3] But the in-the-between factor is nonsubstantialistic. And, Plato says: "He put soul in the center and diffused it through the whole and enclosed everything in it."[4]

This Platonic trinitarianism concerning ultimate things was carried forward by both Plotinus and Proclus in expressions that are theologically precise in relation to Christian theology. Plotinus's Greek is the same as the church's formula: *mia ousia en trisin hypostasesin* (one being in three hypostases).[5] Plotinus explains this in another of his *Enneads:* "May he come bringing his own universe with all the gods that dwell in it — he who is one god and all the gods, where each is all, blending into a unity, distinct in powers, but all one God in virtue of that one divine power with many facets. . . . This is the one God who is all gods."[6] And in yet another place he writes, *doxei ta tria hen einai* (it seems that three are one). But then Plotinus asks rhetorically, "But what is the third?" He answers succinctly: *Psychē*, that is, Soul.[7] To be sure, when this pagan philosopher develops his trinitarian thinking mythologically, the names do not bear family kinship (father, son, etc.), but have Greek appellation (*e.g.*, Uranus, Cronus, and Zeus), and the third term (Zeus) refers to "soul" (*psychē*, not *pneuma* or spirit).[8] The names may be changed, but surely the spirit is the same.

Proclus continues the Platonic trinitarianism. In *The Elements of Theology*, he writes, "Every divine order has an eternal unity of threefold origin."[9] E. R. Dodds, in his commentary on Proclus's *Elements*, demonstrates the retention of this Platonic-Plotinian-Proclean trinitarianism in Christian Neoplatonic theology by citing Pseudo-Dionysius, Psellus, and Erigena.[10] There is indeed a substantial, if often neglected, tradition of *prisca theologica* (ancient theology) in which the ghost of Hekate reigns as perspective, thanks to Plato and his cadre.

The tradition of *prisca theologica*, especially Neoplatonic in mode and substance, had as one of its unifying factors the concern to see connections between pagan mythology and Christian doctrine.[11] Of particular interest in this regard seems to have been the attention to the Trinity. This doctrine, in its Hekatean shape, was traced to a time before Plato, to Hermes Trismegistus (misdated), to Pythagoras, and to Orpheus.[12] Since this last figure was taken to be the ultimate source, the theology was often called Orphic.[13]

Following Plato, Plotinus, and Proclus, the ghostly trinitarian view was articulated in a Christian form by the so-called Dionysius the Areopagite in the sixth century,[14] from whom it was carried forward in the Neoplatonic form by John of Damascus in the eighth century, John Scotus Erigena in the ninth,[15] Michael Psellus in the eleventh,[16] Ramon Lull in the fourteenth,[17] and a host of thinkers in the Renaissance, including Francesco Giorgi, Henry Cornelius Agrippa, Albrecht Dürer, Marsilio Ficino, Agostino Steucco, Guy Lefèvre de la Boderie, Cardinal Bessarion, Philippe Duplessis Mornay, and Paul Beurrier.[18] It culminated in the British Platonism of the eighteenth century, in, for example, the work of Andrew Michael Ramsay and Ralph Cudworth,[19] not to mention that of the scientist Isaac Newton[20] and the poet Edmund Spenser.[21]

But this is not yet the complete list! The fourth-century Neoplatonic theologian, Marius Victorinus, drew on Platonic sources (*i.e.*, the triad of existence, life, and intelligence) for his interpretation of Christian doctrine, as did Bonaventure in the thirteenth century. The work of Pierre Hadot and Ewert Cousins in this regard are particularly helpful to understanding.[22]

The triadic thinking of Gnosticism is closely linked to, and may well be a partial source of, much of this Neoplatonic theology. For example, in "The Apocryphon of John" there is an abundance of important trinities: youth/old man/servant; father/mother/son; father-mother/first man/holy spirit; thrice-male; will/thought/life; grace/truth/form; conception/perception/memory; understanding/love/idea; perfection/peace/sophia; and Yaltabaoth/Saklas/Samael! There are even more trinities in other Gnostic documents: spirit/fire/water, in "On the Origin of the World"; hidden one/first appearing/self-begotten one, and existence/blessedness/life, in "Zostrianus"; and father-mother/son-voice/sound-logos, in "Trimorphic

Protennoia."[23] There may well be more to the Trinity than orthodox theologians have begun to imagine!

The point seems to be that Christian theologizing which has retained a Platonic perspective has also not lost a sense for the mystery of the Trinity and for a trinitarian way of thinking. There is indeed a substantial, if neglected and repressed, tradition which finds the Trinity in all things and all things in the Trinity. A mythological and psychological understanding from antiquity was applied to Christian doctrine, and the Christian imagery was seen to amplify concretely Neoplatonic ideas.[24] Marsilio Ficino wrote, "The Pythagorean philosophers [i.e., the Orphic tradition] believed that a trinity was the measure of everything,[25] for the reason, I think, that God governs things in threes."[26] Another in this line of thinkers (Postel) wrote, "There is no doubt that Plato would have revealed much more about the Holy Trinity, namely, what he had learned from the Prophets [in Egypt], if he had not had scruples about publishing sacred mysteries, which he had acquired with difficulty and wished to keep to himself."[27]

What the church has allowed Neoplatonic theology to keep to itself by ignoring this esoteric tradition and not encouraging its teaching are two insights concerning the traditional theological formulae of the Trinity. One has to do with the Western terminology (personae, three persons); and the other has to do with the Eastern terminology (hypostaseis, three "hypostases"). We turn to the Western formula first.

Noteworthy in the Neoplatonic view of the Trinity is the marrying of the Hekatean notion of angelos (angel) to the "persons" of the Trinity, thereby retaining the notion of ghostly invisible power as messenger or giver of images.[28] The images and forms of ultimate reality come to us by way of ghostly and sometimes ghastly angelic intrusions in which life's limits are experienced as triangular, even though these experiences, as we noted in chapter 3, may seem more "trivial" than divine.

There has long been a tradition in Christendom that the Holy Trinity is composed of three angels, but it has for the most part been forgotten. Jean Daniélou, in a remarkable piece of research, "Trinity and Angelology in Judaeo-Christian Theology," has demonstrated

that three angels was the most common form of the Trinity until the
fourth century when theologians philosophized it with the notions of
persons and hypostases.[29] The Tropici among Egyptian Christians —
so called because of their "figurative" interpretation of Scripture
(*tropos* = trope or figure) — still held to the angel view of the Trinity
in the fourth century, though Athanasius did his best to suppress this
perspective.[30] In spite of the efforts of this bishop, the Eastern church,
and especially the art and iconography of its people, has continuously
depicted the Trinity as three angels.[31]

The intuition that the Trinity is composed of angels has a very
important religious significance. In religions of radical monotheism,
or whenever in life ultimate reality is imagined to be beyond our ability to grasp (that is, when God is unspeakable and unthinkable, a
*deus absconditus*), mediating forms and images, patterns of eternal
meaning, are crucial. As Plato spoke of the necessity of the Third,
and as this book has argued the necessity of the "third" in matters of
love and marriage as a concrete image of trinity, so Neoplatonist theologians spoke of "the necessity of angelology."[32] Without angels there
could be no knowledge of God. Angels are the images of God's
form,[33] and since ultimate reality is believed to be and is experienced
as trinitarian for pagan and Christian alike, one looks to *three* angels
as the shape of that threshold between the one god which is unknown
and unknowable and the gods whose form has lost a ghostly quality.

The necessity of angels can be put succinctly. On the one hand,
without angels as mediating images of immortal meaning, the Holy
Other may be misunderstood supernaturalistically and transcenden-
tally as not being near the self's understanding of itself, there being
imagined an infinite qualitative distinction between man and God
who is therefore now *wholly* other. But on the other hand, if the
mediating forms of meaning are not angelic, like the ghosts of many-
headed Hekate, our meanings may become fixated, walled in, sub-
stantialized, objectivized into monolithic ideas, ideologies, and theological idolatries.[34] The angels, to borrow the words of Curtis
Bennett, "pitch eternity to the shapes which human response makes
of experience."[35] It is as if the angels make metaphors of experience,
making it possible to see meaning in experience that is, though all too
human, nonetheless far more than personal.

The point is put perhaps more plainly by Henry Corbin in his essay
"On the Necessity of Angelology." There he draws attention to Deut.

5:7, where it is written, "You shall have no other Gods before my Face." Corbin connects this text with Neoplatonic angelology.

> Yes, but what is this Face? It would be a matter of that about which it is said: "You shall not see my Face, for no man sees me and lives" (Exodus 33:20). Yet, it is precisely a matter of the Face that God shows to man, his theophany, and the Angel of the Face, all the Angels of the Face, are his theophanies . . . these theophanies of which the transformations correspond to the state and mode of being of those to whom they are shown, face to Face.[36]

So, in Isa. 63:9, when we read the phrase, "the Angel before his Face," it may mean *the image* by which one sees the God who is hidden and yet manifest in our midst. The "secret," says Corbin, is that the phrase "You shall have no other Gods before my Face" comes to mean, "You shall have no other Gods before my Angel."[37] Angels are images, and soul's images are our angels.

C. S. Lewis spoke of this in another way: "When the time comes to you at which you will be forced at last to utter the speech which has lain at the center of your soul for years, which you have, all that time, idiot-like, been saying over and over, you'll not talk about joy of words. I saw well why the Gods do not speak to us openly, nor let us answer. Till that word can be dug out of us, why should they hear the babble that we think we mean? How can they meet us face to face till we have faces?"[38]

The angels are our faces, our images, those limit-experiences which we must face. And facing these as angels, our boundary-experiences may be seen as thresholds of life.[39] Hekate knows the depth of this insight, for in her dark underworldly way of soul, she is called *angelos*, which also may be why she can be called *triprosopos*, "three faces" of one goddess. *Triprosopos* — this name of the goddess Hekate — is of course the very name given by the Western church to the Holy Trinity (*una substantia, tres personae*), for in the beginning *persona* did not mean person but was a synonym for *prosopon*, face. The angelic Hekatean trinity is the mythos of the Three Faces of God . . . Father, Son, and Ghost. Such is what a person must face . . . the ghastly triangle deep within the self, but seen as a threshold (*prothyraia*). Did not Jesus say, "I am the door"?[40]

The Eastern church had a different idea and image. Where the West said *persona* and *prosopon*, meaning face, the East said *hypostasis*, which is ordinarily translated to mean substance. Augustine complained that he did not understand this word,[41] perhaps because its philosophical usage is so abstract. Yet the word was neither philosophical nor abstract in its original sense.

From the time of Plotinus, the Neoplatonists had said that *hypostasis*, like *persona*, was to be understood as "image" (*eikonos*).[42] But in alchemical traditions which were closely associated with Neoplatonism there is an even more concrete clue that connects with an earlier meaning.

Before the word *hypostasis* meant either image or substance, it referred simply to "that which settles (*stasis*) to the bottom (*hypo*)." Early Greek speech used the term to mean an accumulation of pus, a thickening of blood in a wound, jelly, clouds, thick soup, sediment in urine, the foundation of a temple, excrement, wealth (as in our use of the word substance to mean riches), and the lees in the bottom of a wine bottle! A Hebrew psalm says, "Save me, O God! For the waters have come up to my neck. I sink in deep mire and there is no foothold."[43] Greek translators rendered this passage: "I sink in deep mire and there is no *hypostasis*."

Thus, ancient alchemy could use the word *hypostasis* to refer with precision to the process of *coagulatio*. Zosimos of Panapolis, for example, spoke of the trinitarian embodiment (the *hypostases*) of the nameless one, the mystical man who is three (*trias he akatonomastos*). The three hypostases of such a one, he said, were *theos* (god), *angelos* (angel), and *anthropos pathetos* (the man who suffers).[44] The word *hypostasis* still carried this fundamental alchemical sense when the church's fathers, a century after Zosimos, were formulating doctrine: one God, three coagulations!

This alchemical basis to the Christian doctrine of the Trinity has been systematically ignored. To my knowledge it has not once been mentioned in the Western orthodox theological tradition, likely because theology typically attends to concepts rather than images. Yet the alchemical implication in the *language* of traditional theological formulae is clear. The deep mire which man suffers is triangular. It is, the Christian believes, the Trinity. And this mire is ultimate and eternal. Ultimately it is our angel . . . a foothold at the threshold of the door.

In the very passage from Plato which, at Eranos in 1940, set Jung to thinking about the Trinity (see interlude, part 1), there is talk about coagulation. Plato, speaking about the "body" of the cosmos, says not only that "two things alone . . . cannot properly be conjoined without a third," but also that the third, as the connecting function between two things, creates "corporality," "visibility," and "tangibility."[45] Commenting on this passage, the alchemical text known as *Turba philosophorum* states, "God hath created all things by his word, and he said unto them, Be, and they were made with four elements — earth, water, air, and fire — which He coagulated."[46]

The creation of *a* world or of *the* world has often been expressed by religious myths in terms of a coagulation which emerges out of a sort of watery, fluxing chaos. This account, for example, is from Japanese mythology:

> Before the heavens and the earth came into existence, all was chaos, unimaginable, limitless, and without shape or form. Aeon followed aeon: then, lo! out of this boundless, shapeless mass something light and transparent rose up and formed the heaven. In the meantime, what was heavy and opaque in the void gradually precipitated and became the earth, but it had taken an immeasurably long time before it condensed sufficiently to form solid ground.[47]

Mircea Eliade has collected numerous of these "earth diver"-type accounts of creation and creativity.[48]

A similar use of the Neoplatonic and alchemical notion of coagulation has been employed in contemporary depth psychology, in which the creation of *a* world creatively is also at stake. The "world" in this case is, of course, the world of self as a new creation. For example, in the writings by Patricia Berry and James Hillman on dream-psychology and therapy, we read:

> We might image the dream as a series of superimpositions, each event adding texture and thickening to the rest. . . . Dreams are like knots of condensed implications.[49]

> Dreams are made by a coagulative process: condensation, intensification (over-determination), reduction (abbreviation), iteration (repetition), concretizing. The synthetic cooking operation of the dream-work . . . brings disparate ingredients together and concocts them into new things. These dream things we call *symbols*. They are made, or given, as densities, and the German word *Dicht* ("dense," "thick," "tight") occurs both in *Verdichtung* (Freud's term, which we translate as "condensation") and in *Dichtung* ("poetry"), *Dichter* ("poet").[50]

The more general therapeutic point about this dream-psychology of coagulation is made by Hillman when he reports on a comment he made to a patient just after the patient had made a particularly important breakthrough. "I remarked," Hillman says, "about the *coagulatio* of the soul in alchemy: its becoming thickened, sensed as a presence. This had evidently happened like a chemical process. After long cooking, stirring, and containing, suddenly, as in making a sauce, a coagulation takes place."[51] Something similar had happened in the life and the therapy of the patient.

As Edward Edinger has noted,[52] Jung, too, spoke of the importance of *coagulatio* in the creation of the world of the soul (*psyche*). For example, in April of 1929, Jung wrote a letter which makes the alchemical-theological point about coagulation.

> Where God is nearest the danger is greatest. God wants to be born in the flame of man's consciousness. . . . And what if this has no roots in the earth? . . . One must be able to suffer God. . . . He must be the advocate of the earth. . . . God needs man in order to become conscious, just as he needs limitation in time and space, an earthly tabernacle.[53]

Then, in another letter thirty-one years later, Jung wrote:

> I am . . . walking through the dough at the bottom of the sea. . . . This dough, however, is the human mind, as it has been for several thousand years. Being a physician, I am concerned with the woes of the world. . . . I have to help man, who sticks in the dough. In order to help his suffering, I must understand his "dough." . . . I am weak and stupid enough to consider a certain amount of compassion, humility, love, and feeling as indispensable for the understanding of the human soul and its woeful dough, i.e., the slime and mud at its bottom.[54]

As Martin Ruland's *Lexicon* says, the alchemical process of coagulation is called by the name "concretion."[55] One ultimate reality, three concretions! — one of whom is a ghost.

This Neoplatonic and alchemical understanding is brought to articulation by the ancient Pythagorean mathematician, Nichomachus of Gerasa, in his work on "theological arithmetic." He writes: "As the rennet coagulates the running milk by its active and effective property, so the unifying force of the monad approaching the dyad . . . gave a boundary and a form that is a number to the triad."[56] There could not be a more forceful statement of the trinity as coagulations than this second-century text. And for Nichomachus, rennet is the secret.

Rennet is now used for making cheese, ice cream, and gelatin. It is the coagulant and takes its name from the German word "rennen," meaning to run, or in this case, to run together, as in the phrase "mit dem Kopfe gegen eine Sache rennen" (to run one's head against something). Rennet, the protein enzyme that turns the casein in milk to cheese, is extracted from the lining of the stomachs of unweaned calves. It turns the material liquid into body, as the stomach's digestive process does. While many substitutes have been sought for the rennet from the lining of an animal's stomach (fig sap, barley, gook grass, and chemicals) nothing gives body like the stomach of true animality.

There is precedent for joining the coagulation of rennet to theological ideas. In the fifteenth century, the biblical passage about manna from heaven was commented on in this sentence: "The dew of heaven fell on the herbs, and there it coagulated and waxed white."[57] Coagulations are manna from heaven. They are the food of the gods. In the seventeenth-century writings of John Donne, repentance and remission of sin (the confession of hurt about which we spoke with regard to Hekatean suffering) are spoken of as "the rennet which coagulates the body of Christ into a Church."[58]

But apparently these are not the only coagulating forces in human life. Walter Charleton, writing still in Donne's lifetime, spoke of "a Bawd who was the very Rennet of Concupiscence,"[59] as if eros were a coagulant of body and body a coagulant of eros. When love relationships are seen in terms of triangles, our plots thicken!

Indeed, when Edward Edinger comments on the fact that for the alchemists, in addition to magnesia, lead, and honey, sulfur and heat were also agents of coagulation, he says, forthrightly, "desire coagulates."[60] It is like Hekate's eros, and like the eros of our various triangles. These are *coagmentare*, joining, gluing, and cementing. They are — as Jung said about the eros that coagulates[61]— the soul in life and the life of soul. As eros is ultimately and deeply triangular, so we may also suppose Neoplatonically that the trinity is an image of the coagulation of eros.

If we can understand the fundamental triangularity of love, with a little help from alchemy and Neoplatonism it should not be too difficult to understand that any god, who is love, would have to be a trinity.

PART THREE

# LOVING BY
# TRIANGULATION

# 5

## TIGERS
## AND GHOSTS
### The Trinity in
### Modern Secular Literature

Part 1 of this work was occupied with a remembering, in a particular way, of the theological idea of trinity. It was a putting together of the trinitarian idea by attending to the idea's imagery. The occupation of the Trinity turned out to be a preoccupation with eros—with imagery of love and marriage as metaphors of the divine, as figures of ultimacy. But the love always contained a third that makes the relationship possible, even if by haunting it. Where two are one, ultimately there are three.

That this preoccupation, this continuing archetypal imagery of the trinitarian idea in religion, is complex and deep, even tragic and ghastly, was discovered in part 2. There the imagery of the theological idea was probed in terms of its mythic counters, with Hekate presiding, and Neoplatonic angels and alchemy's cheese informing the understanding of a Hekatean presidency and presence. Love is liminal, and ultimately so. We are all betwixt and between.

So much for "faith seeking understanding" (*fides quaerens intellectum*). There still remains an important step, namely, for the understanding to seek life in real life. That is what, in the introduction, was referred to as loving (what Augustine called amor). It will not suffice, we there argued, to be "led back into" (remembering) and "led down into" (contemplating) the images of archetypal theological ideas if love still be lacking. No love, no link to life. In love, with its amorous impulse and passion to think and to feel connections, soul discovers body. Psyche finds amor (eros) at last.

Nor is it easy to love the Trinity, to love trinitarianly, by triangulation. How is it possible to accept the ultimate "fact" of a third in our relationships—relationships with an other, with others, and with

other aspects of ourselves? How can we embrace and accept the deep
ultimate reality of the trinity of Zeus, Hera, and always another? of
the ghastly spirit of Hekate, bewitching our most profound passions?
No wonder the Trinity is, as we noted from the start, an offense to
reason, a stumbling block to belief, and a folly in experience! How
can we connect with that which in this book has been put together
(remembered theologically) and reflected upon (contemplated
mythologically)?

It is at this point that the poets may be crucial in leading the
Trinity through into life. Poetry, by way of metaphors, dramatizes
lifelikenesses, "erweckten sie uns . . . ein Gleichnis" (awakening a
likeness in us), showing the connections by seeing through the images'
ideas. This "seeing through" is critical in religion, and it is guaranteed
in religion by the particular rhetoric of religion — parable, allegory,
analogy, similitude, correspondence, and symbol. In short, trinitarian iconoclasm can be guaranteed if and whenever our understandings are poetized.

Without the poetizing of the Trinity, any talk of the Trinity would
remain binitarian, this or that, either/or, with the third still lacking.
Without the poetics of trinity, our remembering will be mere historicism and our contemplating mere mythologizing, mere doctrinal theologizing or mere pietistic theologizing, mere thought still split from
mere feeling, classical theology and romantic religion with no connection and no transcendence of the dualistic division between mind
and heart. Theopoetic — theology viewed as poetry — can save us from
our idolatries and fixations, which, even if correct, may well remain
regressive.

Nor have contemporary writers of fiction, verse, and drama failed
to note this. Indeed, though the Trinity is honored only in the breach
of piety and doctrine by religion's orthodox traditions, the ultimate
triangularity of being and experience is over and over given testimony, and insistently so, by poets. We will notice that a secular
"theological" perspective, radically Neoplatonic in its mode, is alive
and well in our time, as we review briefly the modern literary testimony in this chapter — Cervantes, Robert Browning, John Keats,
and T. S. Eliot; D. H. Lawrence, James Thurber, and Robert Creeley;
Theodore Roethke, Jorge Luis Borges, Wallace Stevens, and Georg
Trakl; Robert Pirsig, James Joyce, and Edmond Jabès! Trinity redivi-
vus, in culture if not in religion, embracing and accepting poetically

that which is impossible: the suffering and liminality of love, where oneness means three, and where a third makes oneness possible with feeling.

Of course, great care must be taken at this point, the point at which poetry is used in relation to theology. Theopoetic is not lacking in absurdities. We have already noted (p. 75) the warning by Justus George Lawler of "heavy-handedness," wherein the mere spotting of three of anything in a poem sets off triadic and trinitarian tics in the theologian attuned to or, rather, not so well attuned to, poetry.[1] The warning is well taken when one remembers what Ernst Curtius and Maureen Quilligan tell us concerning the "poetic" imagination of theologians in the Middle Ages: that the fact that we all write using three fingers is proof of the Trinity.[2]

James Thurber, who helped modern men and women to laugh at so much that is taken seriously, also noted the absurdity in interpreting literature. In his short story "*What* Cocktail Party?" that refers to T. S. Eliot's *The Cocktail Party*, Thurber begins with the following dialogue:

> "I'm not so stupid as to believe that the cocktail party in 'The Cocktail Party' is actually a cocktail party," Grace Sheldon told me the other day at a cocktail party that was unquestionably a cocktail party. "What do *you* think it is?"[3]

T. S. Eliot's play surely gave rise to much projected meaning, and not a little of it by Christian critics. Thurber parodies this sort of infelicity with a trinitarian fantasy (or is it a parody?).

> "What do *you* think the play is about? What do *you* think it means?" asked Betty.
>
> I decided to withdraw down a murky bypass. "The identity of the third murdered in 'Macbeth' has puzzled Shakespearean scholars for more than three centuries," I said. "Would it impair or increase your pleasure in the great tragedy if you found out who he actually is, or was?"
>
> "It wouldn't make any difference to me," Betty said.
>
> "What are you driving at, Thurber?" asked Tom.
>
> "The Catonian Trium," I said. " 'The Cocktail Party' is plainly a revaluation of the theory of Cato the Elder that two primary identities can sustain an unidentifiable third. That is, the *duum* differs from the *unum* in that it can absorb, without distortion of meaning, the introductions of an unknown, or mysterious, or debatable third."
>
> "Naturally," said Tom with crisp impatience. "Everybody knows that,

but it doesn't apply here. You are adding the Psychiatrist to Julia and Alex when as a matter of fact, *they* are added to him. You don't seem to understand what identity is being concealed."

I found myself in the embarrassing position of being routed in an argument involving a theory I had made up.[4]

Made up?! It is the argument of Plato and Neoplatonic theologians concerning the Trinity! And, in fact, it may well be the dramatic function, or at least one of the dramatic functions, of Eliot's modern play. But Thurber manages to assert it in a humorous story which makes fun of all such sorts of interpretive assertions. He constructs the meaning in a manner that allows it to deconstruct on its own, iconoclastically, in a laugh, like the haunting presence of the absent ghost of Hekate. Wallace Stevens said, "Poetry is a pheasant disappearing in the brush."[5] Poetic understanding deconstructs itself, which is why the poetic mode is so important to theology: so that idolatry may be avoided, and so that religious understanding may be located trinitarianly—"the ghosts of ghosts."[6]

As Thurber has managed to heed Lawler's warning, so have others. Lawler himself mentions the case of Earl Reeves Wasserman who discovered and sensitively showed the threefold structure in the poetry of John Keats.[7] Elizabeth Bieman has managed an impressive demonstration of "Triads and Trinity in the Poetry of Robert Browning."[8] She notes that "the danger of over-schematizing must be resisted," but does not allow this danger to keep her from reporting what is clear in the poetry, namely, that "triadic patterns of thought mark Browning's poetry," and that "he has the company of most Christians in the Pauline, Augustinian and existentialist tradition . . . in making will an agency in bridging the gap." Especially important in the context of the present argument is Bieman's placing of Browning's trinitarian poetic in a Neoplatonic context, and her retention of the insight that the "third is elusive," and always.[9]

Nor are Wasserman and Bieman alone. Ortega y Gassett, meditating on the work of Cervantes, and D. H. Lawrence, reflecting on his own writing, have both stressed the importance of the third in poetics, not to mention the importance of poetic understanding for making sense of the third. Like Browning and like Keats, both Ortega and Lawrence place themselves Platonically in trinitarian understanding.

In *Meditations on Quixote,* Ortega writes:

> When the man of great faith says that he sees God in the flowery fields and in the arch of the night sky, he does not express himself more metaphorically than if he should speak of having seen an orange. If there were only a passive way of seeing, the world would be reduced to a chaos of luminous dots; but besides the passive way there is an active seeing which interprets by seeing and sees by interpreting, a seeing which is observing. Plato found a divine word for these visions which come from observing: he called them ideas. Just as the third dimension of the orange is only an idea, God is the ultimate dimension of the countryside. . . . Vision is depth.[10]

We can see the length and the breadth of an object, but the third dimension, the dimension of depth, is imagined and is imaginal in nature. Yet, it is just this imaginal depth and this profound imagination, an active imagination to be sure, that is the precondition of understanding . . . oranges and divinity. Don Quixote knew!

And so does D. H. Lawrence, who is more explicit than Ortega in marking the connection between a Platonic poetics and the Christian notion of the Trinity. Lawrence is writing about "the vicious circle" of how a person knows anything, the sort of dynamic referred to in our century as "the hermeneutic circle." Like Ortega, he is expressing the fantasy of the importance of fantasy, or poetic imagination, for all of our knowings. "The soul," Lawrence says, "is forever an unknowable reality."

> There is a continual conflict between the soul, which is forever sending forth incalculable impulses, and the psyche, which is conservative, and wishes to persist in its old motions, and the mind, which wishes to have "freedom," that is spasmodic, idea-driven control. Mind, and conservative psyche, and the incalculable soul, these three are a trinity of powers in every human being.[11]

Thus far Lawrence seems to be speaking of tritheism, of three *things*, rather than of a trinitarian understanding in which three are one by virtue of a ghostly third which is not a thing.

But Lawrence takes the additional step in the direction of trinitarian insight, saying that "there is something beyond these" three powers in every human being.

> It is the individual in his pure singleness, in his totality of consciousness, in his oneness of being: the Holy Ghost which is with us after our Pentecost, and which we may not deny. When I say to myself, "I am wrong," knowing with sudden insight that I *am* wrong, then this is the whole self speaking, the Holy Ghost. It is no piece of mental inference. It is

not just the soul sending forth a flash. It is my whole being speaking in one voice, soul and mind and psyche transfigured into oneness. This voice of my being I may *never* deny.[12]

Elsewhere, Lawrence refers to this as a person's "blood-consciousness."[13] But, by whatever name, the perspective (and here also, the terminology) is trinitarian.

Lawrence makes his opinion clear about the poetic principle, what he calls "fantasia."

> We must live by all three, ideal, impulse, and tradition, each in its hour. But the real guide is the pure conscience, the voice of the self in its wholeness, the Holy Ghost. . . . In China, it is tradition. And in the South Seas, it seems to have been impulse. Ours is idealism. Each of the three modes is a true life-mode. But any one, alone or dominant, brings us to destruction. We must depend on the wholeness of our being, ultimately only on that, which is our Holy Ghost within.[14]

The Holy Ghost, the incalculable soul, the poetic imagination — such is the nature of the third which is the life-connection. A poem is the Holy Ghost in its function of linking idea and life, tradition and reality, myth(ology) and psyche(ology). Poetry is clue to the Trinity . . . as it "disappears into the brush."

It is just this iconoclastic "pheasant," this deconstructive principle that disallows certain literature from our consideration, even though a third and three things be invoked. For example, triadic tics may well be sent into spasm by this delicious verse by Robert Creeley:

> I dreamt. I saw three ladies in a tree,
> and the one that I saw most clearly
> showed her favors unto me,
> and I saw her leg above the knee!
>
> But when the time for love was come,
> and of readiness I had made myself,
> upon my head and shoulders
> dropped the other two like an unquiet dew.
>
> What were these two but the one?
> I saw in their faces, I heard in their words,
> wonder of wonders! it was the undoing of me
> they came down to see!
>
> Sister, they said to her who upon my lap
> sat complacent, expectant:
> he is dead in his head, and we
> have errands, have errands . . .

> O song of wistful night! Light shows
> where it stops nobody knows, and two
> are one, and three, to me, and to look
> is not to read the book.
>
> *Oh one, two, three! Oh one, two, three!*
> *Three old ladies sat in a tree.*[15]

The eros we have learned to expect in trinitarian matters, the three-someness we have come to expect in matters of love, is certainly present in this poem. But to find a trinity here (other than that of Aeschylus's Furies or Shakespeare's weird sisters) would simply be to leave the poem and its poetic, and to engage in the worst form of theological criticism, a bringing of theolog*ism* to poem rather than poetic to theology.

Lines from T. S. Eliot's *The Wasteland* may be, if less erotic, nonetheless more tempting to the trinitarian seeking lifelikenesses for a psycho-mythological theology.

> Who is the third who walks always beside you?
> When I count, there are only you and I together
> But when I look ahead up the white road
> There is always another one walking beside you
> Gliding wrapt in a brown mantle, hooded
> I do not know whether a man or a woman
> —But who is that on the other side of you?[16]

This seems a likely candidate for our consideration in a theopoetic of the Trinity. The third is properly ghostly ("hooded") and its function is to connect (here through interrogation) two others the *white* road and "walking" point to the processionism of persons and the *other-*worldly dimension of reality seen through prisms of ultimacy.

But there is still a matter that serves to discount Eliot's lines. The author himself tells in a footnote that this verse refers to the journey to Emmaus. As the New Testament says:

> That very day two of them were going to a village named Emmaus, about seven miles from Jerusalem, and talking with each other about all these things that had happened. While they were talking and discussing together, Jesus himself drew near and went with them. But their eyes were kept from recognizing him.[17]

To be sure, Eliot does not mention Jesus in the text of the poem itself. He is not as theologically explicit as Lawrence, who uses the phrase "Holy Ghost." Yet Eliot is theological in a way that Lawrence is not, and the allegorical theologism (with its explicit footnote by the author) displaces the Hekatean perspective of the Trinity in favor of an irony — they do not recognize the ghost, as if Christ in our time is not only a ghost but is "the ghost of a ghost"— an irony which carries a certainty concerning fixed meanings. That is, this poem does not deconstruct at all. The pheasant is, so to speak, out in the open, even if ironically. The third is present, but as a theological some-*thing*. The subject is trinitarian, but the perspective is not. It is binitarian theology, not poetry, even if it appears in verse form.

What we are seeking in a trinitarian poetic is something a good deal more subtle than Creeley, on the one hand, and than Eliot, on the other. Instances from Theodore Roethke, Jorge Luis Borges, Wallace Stevens, and Georg Trakl will help make the point.

Roethke's poem is entitled "The Happy Three," although by no means do things begin happily.

> Inside, my darling wife
> Sharpened a butcher knife
> Sighed out her pure relief
>     That I was gone.
>
> When I had tried to clean
> My papers up, between
> Words skirting the obscene —
>     She frowned her frown.
>
> Shelves have a special use;
> And why muddy shoes
> In with your underclothes?
>     She asked, woman.
>
> So I betook myself
> With not one tiny laugh
> To drink some half-and-half
>     On the back lawn.

So it begins: a little drama in the dyad of marriage, a dialogical tension. But . . . "Who should come up right then, . . ." Indeed, who? What is it that comes into such "betweens"? There is already anger as a third in the relationship ("not one tiny laugh"). But how can the two once again realize the oneness?

> Who should come up right then,
> But our goose, Marianne,
> Having escaped her pen,
>     Hunting the sun.

An animal! like the animality of the anger. But a particular animal: a goose! like the silly goose we make of ourselves in such scenes. But the particular animal, this goose, has an even more particular name.

> Named for a poetess,
> (Whom I like none-the-less),
> Her pure-white featheriness
>     She paused to preen;

The poet (presumably Marianne Moore) appears in the "between." The poem is the third—in its ghostly lyrical "pure-white featheriness." The function of this animal/goose/Marianne/poem is nothing other than poetic justice and a justice poetized in a trinitarian manner.

> But when she pecked my toe,
> My banked-up vertigo
> Vanished like April snow;
>     All rage was gone.
>
> . . . . . . . . . . . . .
> Back to the house we ran,
> Me, and dear Marianne—
> Then we romped out again,
>     Out again,
>     Out again,
>     Three in the sun.[18]

The three are one, by virtue of the third which is not like the other two, "pure-white featheriness," a goose ghosting the rage in the poem which expresses it.

Though it is still an animal which is the third, both animal and tone become more serious in the poem of Jorge Luis Borges than they were in Roethke's verse. Borges's poem, "The Other Tiger," opens with an epigram that suggests that the trinitarian dramaturgy in this verse has to do with the art of poetry itself. The epigram is from the work of Morris, "Sigurd the Volsung" (1876): "And the craft that created a semblance."

The poem begins with its author, Borges, sitting sightless in a gloomy library and finding that his dreaming brings life to otherwise lifeless reality.

> I think of a tiger. The gloom here makes
> The vast and busy Library seem lofty
> And pushes the shelves back;

Strong, innocent, covered with blood and new,
It will move through its forest and its morning
And will print its tracks on the muddy
Margins of a river whose name it does not know
(In its world there are no names nor past
Nor time to come, only the fixed moment)
And will overleap barbarous distances
And will scent out of the plaited maze
Of all the scents the scent of dawn
And the delighting scent of the deer.
Between the stripes of the bamboo I decipher
Its stripes and have the feel of the bony structure
That quivers under the glowing skin.
In vain do the curving seas intervene
And the deserts of the planet;
From this house in a far-off port
In South America, I pursue and dream you,
O tiger on the Ganges' banks.

The actual tiger (dreamed of) in India is the first of three, and its
actuality is concretely powerful (in dream)—"blood," "muddy," "barbarous," "scent," "glowing skin." But the poet, in crafting for the
poem what is already a reality only in dream, then begins to reflect
on that real tiger now told of in verse.

In my soul the afternoon grows wider and I reflect
That the tiger invoked in my verse
Is a ghost of a tiger, a symbol,
A series of literary tropes
And memories from the Encyclopaedia
And not the deadly tiger, the fateful jewel
That, under the sun or the varying moon,
In Sumatra or Bengal goes on fulfilling
Its round of love, of idleness and death.
To the symbolic tiger I have opposed
The real thing, with its warm blood,
That decimates the tribe of buffaloes
And today, the third of August, '59,
Stretches on the grass a deliberate
Shadow, but already the fact of naming it
And conjecturing its circumstance
Makes it a figment of art and no creature
Living among those that walk the earth.

It would seem that this is the end of it!—the real tiger (albeit
dreamed), and the tiger written about as image and metaphor in "the

craft that createth a semblance" (albeit in a literally actual text). But
it is not yet the end.

> We shall seek a third tiger. This
> Will be like those others a shape
> Of my dreaming, a system of words
> A man makes and not the vertebrate tiger
> That, beyond the mythologies,
> Is treading the earth. I know well enough
> That something lays on me this quest
> Undefined, senseless and ancient, and I go on
> Seeking through the afternoon time
> The other tiger, that which is not in verse.[19]

The third is elusive, but it is that which will link dream and reality,
word and spirit, in the interpsychic drama where meaning is eventful
and where "the other tiger," the third haunting the quest, makes realities of ghosts by ghosting the realities tigrously. The craft of semblance, graced by "the other tiger," is the poetizing of meaning
"beyond mythologies."

It is the craft of poetry (language) that is at stake in Wallace
Stevens's work, too, although at first it may appear that the marriage
of actual everyday life, as opposed to the "marriage" of dream and
reality in individual consciousness, is the subject of his trinitarian
insight. For, beyond Roethke's goose and Borges's tiger there flies
Stevens's blackbird, invoked in chapter 2.

> A man and a woman
> Are one.
> A man and a woman and a blackbird
> Are one.[20]

Simple and straightforward, and by now in this book's argument,
Stevens's blackbird can function as a summary.

Yet, we must not be tempted to think that we now somehow understand the poetry of the Trinity, which is, after all, an ultimate mystery. That there may be more than we think we know in Stevens's
haiku-like Zennish poem is perhaps indicated with his three-stanza
verse called "Nomad Exquisite" which follows the blackbird in
Stevens's *Collected Poems*.

> As the immense dew of Florida
> Brings forth
> The big-finned palm

And green vine angering for life,
As the immense dew of Florida
Brings forth hymn and hymn
From the beholder,
Beholding all these green sides
And gold sides of green sides,
And blessed mornings,
Meet for the eye of the young alligator,
And lightning colors
So, in me, come flinging
Forms, flames, and the flakes of flames.[21]

It would appear that, as Stevens's man and woman and blackbird resemble Roethke's husband and wife and goose, so the structure of "Nomad Exquisite" resembles Borges's "The Other Tiger."

First there is immensely actual and fruitful Florida, with its "palm" tree and "green vine." Then, in the second stanza, the poet-"beholder" crafts his writing about this experience of actuality ("hymn and hymn"). But there is something further, a third stanza. In it is a morning which blesses, because one sees now ("the eye") from the perspective of the animal (alligator), a perspective which, though new (young) gives color and fire, the fireworks of the poetry of meaning.

The resemblance between this movement and that of Borges's poem is clear, but there is a difference, too. Borges's animal was feline (tiger), whereas Stevens's bestial imagination is chthonic (alligator); Borges's quest was eastward (Sumatra or Bengal), whereas Stevens's is southward (Florida), "hunting the sun," like Roethke's goose, going toward the "gold sides of green," the flame of poems whose language comes "flinging forms"—fire flakes. Borges's trinitarian insight refers to the language of a deep animal-*consciousness* (a gloomy reflection in a vast library); Stevens's poem seems to be about the *language* of a deep animal-consciousness (hymns flinging forms).

In our quest for a trinitarian poetic, a poetic understanding of the Trinity that will retain the mystery while expressing it, three different themes have emerged. In each instance—Roethke, Borges, and Stevens—there is a drama expressed, what Kenneth Burke would call "a dramatistic logology." But the dramas are not the same.

Roethke's "The Happy Three" is the poetry of a sociological drama. It pictures an everyday marriage scene between two persons, a man and a woman, with the animal-third, a goose named Marianne, pecking the "banked-up vertigo" which, as a result of a third, "vanished like April snow." And the three were one.

Borges's poem, "The Other Tiger," expresses a poetry of psychological dramaturgy. It presents an interior and gloomy reflection concerning epistemic uncertainty: What can I know for sure? And even if I could know something, how could I express it? Between reality and my expressions of it, I seek a third to give a tiger's spirit and life to the whole.

In Stevens's "Nomad Exquisite," the poetry depicts the drama of language. In this poetry about poetry, the procession of verses discloses the exquisite flakes of flame gilding the flinging forms of creative utterance. Language wanders, "nomad." And in its wandering, it receives "lightning colors" as it is imagined actively through "the eye of the young alligator."

Certainly this is more subtle than Eliot's scriptural allegory, and more to the point of the Trinity than Creeley's "Three Ladies." For in Roethke, Borges, and Stevens we see the everyday locations of the Trinity, *vestigia trinitatis*, in external life and in interior life and in the syntax of the very speech by which we represent external and internal events to ourselves and to others. Yet, beyond these instances, there is another which is even subtler and deeper. Whether it is more to the trinitarian point than these first three remains to be seen.

Georg Trakl's poem "A Winter Evening," like the poem by Stevens, has three verses.

> When the snow fell on the window,
> The vesper bell tolled long;
> The table was prepared for many,
> And the house was well provided.
>
> Many persons, on the journey,
> Come to the door by darksome paths.
> The tree of graces blooms in gold
> From out of the cool dew of the earth.
>
> A wanderer steps quietly inside:
> Pain has turned the threshold to stone.
> There, in unalloyed clarity, shown
> Bread and wine on the table.[22]

Martin Heidegger has written a remarkable meditation on this poem. His reflection begins:

> The poem describes a winter evening. The first stanza describes what

is happening outside: snowfall, and the ringing of the vesper bell. The
things outside touch the things inside the human homestead. The snow
falls on the window. The ringing of the bell enters into every house.
Within, everything is well provided and the table set.

The second stanza raises a contrast. While many are at home within
the house and at the table, not a few wander homeless on dark paths.
And yet such — possibly evil — roads sometimes lead to the door of the
sheltering house. To be sure, this fact is not presented expressly. Instead,
the poem names the tree of graces.

The third stanza bids the wanderer enter from the dark outdoors into
the brightness within. The houses of the many and the tables of their
daily meals have become house of God and altar.[23]

By the first stanza of Trakl's poem, the "outside" of external social
relationships seen in Roethke's poem and the "interiority" expressed
in Borges's reflection are commingled in a poetic language not
entirely unlike that of Stevens ("nomad"/"wanderer"; gold of the
green hymns and palms/gold of the tree of graces; flakes of fire fling-
ing/bread and wine shining). The motifs of the poems by Roethke,
Borges, and Stevens are recapitulated in this verse by Trakl, and the
procession of the drama in the direction of a third (what the church
fathers called *perichoresis*, circle dance, in the case of the procession
of persons in the Trinity) is in this instance also similar to those other
three. But there is a new element — pain!

"Schmerz versteinerte die Schwell," Trakl writes in the third
stanza, which literally means "pain stonified the threshold." The
"dark paths" of wandering, the dark "earth" which is the source of
moistening ("dew"), the shadings of nightfall ("vesper bell tolled") —
these images and others like them coagulate experience; and such
concrete renderings of pathos become the "threshold" of the "door,"
the link between inside and out. They are the images, the words of
the poem, which commingle, which marry the polarities of our various oppositions, making a communion ("bread and wine") of life's
"journey." These "darks"— like Wallace Stevens's "hilarious dark" and
his "black sublime," like the superluminous darkness of Western mys-
tics (Dionysius the Areopagite, Bonaventure, St. John of the Cross) —
are the gold blooms of the "tree of graces."[24] Poetry makes its rock,
its cornerstone, in pain; and pain, poetically perceived, is a threshold.
It puts us in the middle, on the boundary. Hera knew! Her tragic
mythos is Hekatean, trinitarianly so. But in Trakl the mythos is
poetized, and the trinitarian insight becomes substantial.

To be sure, there is no explicit mention of *the* Trinity in the poetry
of Roethke, Borges, Stevens, and Trakl. And yet, in another way,
there is more trinity here than in all the literal creeds of Christendom, mouthed but forgotten in a traditional religiosity that has
remained binitarian in practice (God and Jesus) and binitarian in
perspective ("either/or"). For there is deep trinitarian insight in both
the form and the function of these poems. Here, mythopoetically, all
the tradition's trinitarian insistence and intent is intact: eros, pain, a
third of like coagulation yet somehow different, ghostly, a circle
dance, a *ménage à trois*, giving spirit, when three are one, ultimately.
The Trinity-as-perspective is indeed alive and well, even if not
explicit, even if still hidden in deep mystery.

The poets carry the mythos, but in narrative poetics there is a good
deal of trinitarian "theology," too.

Robert M. Pirsig is explicit in *Zen and the Art of Motorcycle Maintenance*. Phaedrus, the "hero," muses late in the novel about "Quality," which is a "quality" missing from thought and feeling, not to
mention life. Is Quality subjective or objective, he wonders?

> Finally: Phaedrus, following a path that to his knowledge had never
> been taken before in the history of Western thought [!], went straight
> between the horns of the subjectivity-objectivity dilemma and said
> Quality is neither a part of mind, nor is it a part of matter. It is a *third*
> entity which is independent of the two.
>
> He was heard along the corridors and up and down the stairs of Mon-
> tana Hall singing softly to himself, almost under his breath, "Holy,
> holy, holy . . . blessed Trinity."
>
> And there is a faint, faint fragment of memory, possibly wrong, possi-
> bly just something I'm imagining, that says he just let the whole
> thought structure sit like that for weeks, without carrying it any
> further.[25]

As the weeks go by, Phaedrus becomes more and more obsessed
with this trinitarian perspective, sensing that such a perspective could
give Quality to existence. Yet he finds it difficult to *think* through.

> Although there's no logical objection to a metaphysical trinity, a three-
> headed reality, such trinities are not common or popular. The metaphy-
> sician normally seeks either a monism, such as God, which explains the
> nature of the world as a manifestation of one single thing, or he seeks
> a dualism, such as mind-matter, which explains it as two things, or he
> leaves it as a pluralism which explains it as a manifestation of an

indefinite number of things. But three is an awkward number. Right
away you want to know, Why three?[26]

So Phaedrus ponders further.

At last he comes to the crux. He knows that most persons believe
Quality is a subjective state. But he also knows that in actual experience, "Quality takes you out of yourself, makes you aware of the
world around you."[27] So it must also be objective, in some sense. Yet,
Quality is not a *tertium quid,* not a some-thing. So Phaedrus concludes: "Quality is not a thing. It is an event. . . . It is the event at
which the subject becomes aware of the object. . . . It is the point
at which subject and object meet."[28] "Believe me," Phaedrus comes to
see, "when the world is seen not as a duality of mind and matter but
as a trinity of quality, mind and matter, then the art of motorcycle
maintenance and other arts take on a dimension of meaning they
never had."[29]

Fine! Yet it all sounds a bit unextraordinary, commonplace, and
abstract. Like so much traditional theology, it is merely assertive,
and, thus far, not much is gained by hearing it from the pages of literary fiction. However, the novelist does not leave it in the empyrean
of mere abstract thought for long. The trinitarian insight takes on a
much different tone when it is applied to the notion of "gumption."
Phaedrus, fifty-six pages later, says:

> I like the word "gumption" because it's so homely and forlorn and so
> out of style it looks as if it needs a friend and isn't likely to reject anyone
> who comes along. It's an old Scottish word, once used a lot by pioneers,
> but which, like "kin," seems to have all but dropped out of use. I like
> it also because it describes exactly what happens to someone who con-
> nects with Quality. He gets filled with gumption.

Phaedrus goes on, clearly filled with gumption by this time, and not
unselfconscious that his secular life is under theological perspective.

> The Greeks called it *enthousiasmos,* the root of "enthusiasm," which
> means literally "filled with *theos,*" a God, or Quality. See how that fits?
>
> A person filled with gumption doesn't sit around dissipating and stew-
> ing about things. He's at the front of the train of his own awareness,
> watching to see what's up the track and meeting it when it comes.
> That's gumption.[30]

But gumption is not mere behavioral activism, either.

> The gumption-filling process occurs when one is quiet long enough to

> see and hear and feel the real universe, not just one's own stale opinions about it.[31]

This quiet is not unlike Trakl's snow at the window which quiets and slows life so that the vesper bell may be heard inside. But the quieting is not, on the other hand, a mere quietism.

> If you're going to repair a motorcycle, an adequate supply of gumption is the first and most important tool. If you haven't got that you might as well gather up all the other tools and put them away, because they won't do any good.[32]

Nor is this trinitarian insight a panacea, a new romanticism for Pirsig. It is important and real just because there are no panaceas in the face of existential pain. So Pirsig ends the novel with this paragraph:

> Trials never end, of course. Unhappiness and misfortune are bound to occur as long as people live, but there is a feeling now, that was not here before, and is not just on the surface of things, but penetrates all the way through. . . . You can sort of tell these things.[33]

And — in a typically Augustinian mood — Pirsig reminds his reader that "the real cycle you're working on is a cycle called 'yourself.' "[34]

James Joyce is less direct than Pirsig. To be sure, "the sacred pigeon" is a leitmotif of *Ulysses*, especially in its function as third when discussed by Stephen in the section on Scylla and Charybdis. And the numerous trigrams in *Finnegans Wake* have clearly trinitarian function in the poetry of the text — IHS (I Have Sinned; I Have Suffered); HCE (Here Comes Everybody; High Church of England; He'll Cheat Erehwon); ALP (Anna Livia Plurabel); etc. But in these two novels especially, there is a much deeper and less obvious trinitarian theme.

The matter is complex, as complex as the strange forms these novels take, but there is no need to labor the matter here, inasmuch as it has been demonstrated most admirably by Richard Ellman,[35] Frank Budgen,[36] and, most thoroughly, in a long study by Phillipe Sollers.[37] Suffice it for our purposes to give two examples so that the difference in level and tone from that of Pirsig may be sensed. Both examples come from *Ulysses*. The first shows the manner in which Joyce muses upon processionism, the parade of persons, in trinity and in life. It sets the problematic of the relation between any twosome.

> Paternity may be a legal fiction. Who is the Father of any Son that any
> Son should love him or he any Son. . . . Sabellius, the African, subtlest
> heresiarch of all the beasts of the field, held that the Father was Himself
> His own Son. The bulldog of Aquin, with whom no word shall be
> impossible, refutes him. Well: if the father who has not a son be not a
> father, can the son who has not a father be a son? When Rutlandbacon-
> southamptonshakespeare or another poet of the same name in the
> comedy of errors wrote HAMLET he was not the father of his own son
> merely, but being no more a son, he was and felt himself the father of
> all his race.[38]

The metaphor of artistic generation (the poet Shakespeare) is
applied here to the enigma of human generation. The third factor
that is needed (as in the trinitarian dispute between Sabellius and
Aquinas) is disclosed in another passage in the same novel, a passage
which seems a parody of the Apostles' creed.

> He Who Himself begot, middler the Holy Ghost, and Himself sent
> Himself, Agenbuyer, between Himself and others, Who, put upon by
> His friends, stripped and whipped, was nailed like bat to barndoor,
> starved on crosstree, Who let Him bury, stood up, harrowed hell, fared
> into heaven and there these nineteen hundred years sitteth on the right
> hand of His Own Self but yet shall come in the latter day to doom the
> quick and dead when all the quick shall be dead already.[39]

The mode here seems as allegorical as Eliot's "who is the third who
walks always beside you," but the tone is qualitatively removed, in the
manner of what Joyce elsewhere calls "the joking Jesus" and the
Trinity "the Libidinous God."[40] With Joyce, "the gaiety of language
is our seigneur"[41] . . . not to mention eros.

Edmond Jabès has picked up both elements, humor, which is not
to be confused with mere wit or cleverness, and eros, which is not
without passion's pain. In his remarkable work *The Book of Questions*, trinitarian insight emerges in Jewish context. Commentary is
as needless as it is impossible.

> Reb Jacob, who was my first teacher, believed in the virtue of the lie
> because, so he said, there is no writing without lie. And writing is the
> way of God. . . .
> Pomp and solemnity are the language of princes. They are the lies of
> men. (Likewise lovers' caresses.) Nakedness, poverty are the lies of God.
> I will tell you about the lie of the rose, the fire contained in its petals.
> (The rose is the most feminine of flowers.) I will tell you about the
> number "3" whose symbol it is. The petals, two at a time, suggest the
> shape of the "3." The corolla and stem form a "9," which is three times

three couples of petals. The hand which plucks the rose and lifts it to the mouth traces, unawares, the voluptuous progress of the number "3."

(Why is the rose the symbol of the number "3"? The narcissus, for example, with its mirror shadow, the anemone regina or the ever green iberis sempervirens with their petals like pairs of butterflies, or even the flower commonly called chickweed: all of them have more claim to this honor. But the rose is the best liar.)

"Three times," said Reb Grisha, "once every three months, the child in the womb kicks against the number 'One,' which is the first letter and which, added to itself (the masculine 'One,' plus the feminine 'One,' plus the masculine-feminine 'One') forms the number 'Three.' 'Three' presides over our fate.

"Man, who is at the same time *being, non-being,* and *super-being,* incarnates it even beyond death."

And Reb Chemtob:

"The one is celebrated three times. For the One and Only is shadow, half-light, and sun."

And Reb Liatob:

"The first letter torments the alphabet. For it is three times itself and three times the letters it introduces."

I will tell you the lie of big numbers and little numbers, the lie of circle and triangle, which are the passages and impasse of sorcery.

I will tell you about the lie of faith which is consumed by flames, which does not lift you, but goes up in smoke. . . .

I will tell you about the third day.[42]

The "lie of circle and triangle," the one who is three and the three that is one, is the truth about God who is a rose!

Surely Ramon Lull would have approved. For he, too, wrote about the circle and triangle, in a trinitarian Christian theology which might have been a Platonic alternative to the Aristotelian orthodoxy of his contemporary, Aquinas. But Lull's work, like the triangle, was rejected in favor of orthodox truth, which has turned out to be a lie. Lull's parable, like Jabès's, is its own interpretation.

It is narrated that Circle, Square, and Triangle met together in Quantity, who was their mother, and who was holding a golden apple. She asked her sons if they knew to which of them the apple should be given. To which Circle replied that he ought to have it because he was the firstborn and was greater and could run more strongly than his brothers. Square said that he ought to have it, because he was nearer to man than Circle, and greater than Triangle. Triangle, on the contrary, said that he should have the apple, because he was nearer to man than Circle, and more like God than Square.

Whereupon Quantity gave the apple to her son Triangle.

> But Aries, and his brothers, and Saturn, and his brothers, reproved Quantity, saying that she had judged wrongly; because Triangle had no likeness to God in length, width, and depth, whereas Circle was like God, because he had no beginning nor end. And Square reproved Quantity saying that she had not judged well because he was more like God in the four elements than was Triangle; for without the four elements there would not be men, who exist in order that they may seek out and know God.
>
> But Triangle excused his mother Quantity, saying that she had judged well, for he was more like the Soul of man and God the Trinity through the ternary number than were his brothers Circle and Square. Yet she had erred somewhat, for she had given him a *round* apple, which was not his figure.[43]

Perhaps she had not erred . . . or perhaps her error was in being Quantity rather than Quality . . . or perhaps they are one in this medieval tale . . . as Hebrew Eve and Hellenic judgment of Paris are in communion here, which is to say, Jew and Greek are one in the Trinity, a trinitarian lesson not easy for a Christianity that little understands the eros of its own ideas, and says, "What has Athens to do with Jerusalem?" Two things one, by way of a third. . . .

Jesus says; "What God hath joined together, let no man put asunder!" (Matt. 19:6). Perhaps this saying refers to the "marriage of heaven and hell," eros and pain. It would take a trinitarian perspective to grasp this, and it is just this that the poetics of trinity *has* grasped: the poets joining together again what theologians have sundered in their dualistic binitarian ways of thinking.

The literary references in this chapter have been brief; as cryptic as the Trinity, and as enigmatic as its perspective. But in each of them — in Thurber, Creeley, and Eliot; in Roethke, Borges, Stevens, and Trakl; in Pirsig, Joyce, Jabès, and Lull — when the trinitarian insight is expressed in literature, there is drama in the verse or narrative, as if the trinitarian insight is itself dramatic.

The possibility that drama is the genre most appropriate to the Trinity leads us to muse a bit further in the next interlude, taking a single author, Harold Pinter, and following in his corpus the differentiations of the trinitarian form and function. It is hoped thereby to gain an even deeper sense of the movement "through," from the psycho-mythological trinitarian imagery into the pathology of everyday life.

Interlude

# PINTERESQUE LOVE
## Triangles in Post-Modern Drama

Poetry is crucial to theology — or so it was argued at the beginning of chapter 5 and in the introduction. "Theopoetic" is the name given to this insight and its perspective, a name coined by Stanley R. Hopper and amplified by Amos N. Wilder.[1]

But in the special case of trinitarian form and function, it is a particular poetic that seems pertinent, namely, that of drama. From Euripides and Aristophanes to Sheridan and Molière, from Shakespeare and Jonson to Albee and Beckett, the *ménage à trois* has been the stock in trade of dramatic art. Drama, in the Western tradition, has been about triangles, as if the triangle in human and not-so-human relationships is fundamentally dramatic.

Two plays by Samuel Beckett, *Play* and *Ghost Trio*, sum up the dramatic tradition of loving by triangulation. They certainly serve well to give dramatic summation to this book's argument concerning the Trinity, inasmuch as they contain the motifs and perspectives herein articulated: the third as the connecting factor, the erotic complicity and thematic, the ghastly and ghostly nature of the third and the threesome, and the three as personae (Neoplatonism and Gnosticism) and coagulations (alchemy).

*Play* was originally performed in 1963 in Germany and one year later in Great Britain. The cast includes three figures: First Woman, Second Woman, and Man. All three are present on the stage from the beginning of *Play* until the end. Each is inside a large grey funeral urn, head protruding, "neck held fast in the urn's mouth," as if now dead though nonetheless lively. There is a "fourth character," yet it is not a character at all. It is a spotlight with a single source as the author dictates, and it must swivel back and forth from one face to the other, as if to suggest a oneness of the three. The broken and tragic story that unfolds among the three, hinted at but never clearly stated, is of a love affair that ended in the death of all.[2]

Thirteen years after the first performance of *Play*, Beckett produced *Ghost Trio* for British television. In this work there is a single voice (Female), while the television audience sees a single figure (Male). The tale is not so different from the first, but it is even less clear. What is "apparent" is the music, which in this production functions as did the spotlight in *Play*. The music is from the largo of Beethoven's Fifth Piano Trio, popularly called "The Ghost Trio." This title has attached itself to the work because of the second movement whose main theme was found in a sketchbook Beethoven had been making for a proposed opera on *Macbeth*. The key is D-minor, the key, as musicologists have observed, of *Sturm und Drang* (storm and stress), associated with romanticism. The musical performance of "The Ghost Trio" is characterized by rather unusual flutters on the piano which are heard intermittently during the second movement.[3]

A close reading of Beckett's pair of productions would be useful in demonstrating the paradox that, though dead, the trinitarian idea is alive in modern drama — dramatically alive. Yet, in the dramatic corpus of another dramatist of our time, Harold Pinter, one can follow the rich variety of trinitarian thematics and, especially, their development in poetic language and dramatic action. What is condensed and compact in Beckett is amplified, and amply so, in Pinter.

But as we proceed to search out the trinitarian form and function in Pinter's dramatic works, care must be taken. We surely do not want to exercise the flatfooted and farfetched hermeneutic of one critic who thought he had discovered the Trinity in Pinter's play, *The Dumbwaiter*, because the gas stove referred to by the characters had three rings![4] This hardly constitutes a reading *of Pinter*, and it is the sort of interpretation that plagues not only Pinter but contemporary "theatre of the absurd" in general.

Pinter, not without a good deal of justice, has complained about this. In 1970, when he was accepting the Shakespeare Prize in Hamburg, Germany, for his plays *Landscape* and *Silence*, he told this story:

> Once, many years ago, I found myself engaged uneasily in a public discussion on the theatre. Someone asked me what my work was 'about.'

I replied with no thought at all and merely to frustrate this line of enquiry: 'The weasel under the cocktail cabinet.' That was a great mistake. Over the years I have seen that remark quoted in a number of learned columns. It has now seemingly acquired profound significance, and is seen to be a highly relevant and meaningful observance about my own work. But for me the remark meant precisely nothing.[5]

This anecdote is reminiscent of Thurber's story "*What* Cocktail Party?" about a cocktail party at which there is a discussion of Eliot's *The Cocktail Party* (see chap. 5). Such talk may well be, indeed, a "weasel under the cocktail cabinet," or a "pheasant disappearing into the brush" (Wallace Stevens). And it may be well to keep in mind that such talk means "precisely nothing." We shall have to keep our eye on this nothing.

But how can one keep an eye on nothing, on the no-thing? Theologians have, of course, been attempting this for centuries, trying to keep an eye on the no-thing which is "God." Pinter gave a poet's-eye view of this task, as he tries to engage in it, in the same speech at Hamburg.

I have found that the image must be pursued with the greatest vigilance, calmly, and once found, must be sharpened, graded, accurately focused and maintained, and that the keyword is economy, economy of movement and gesture, of emotion and its expression, both the internal and the external in specific and exact relation to each other, so that there is no wastage and no mess.[6]

In Bristol, eight years earlier in 1962, Pinter had put the matter in a slightly different way when speaking at the National Student Drama Festival. "I have usually begun a play in quite a simple manner; found a couple of characters in a particular context, thrown them together and listened to what they said, keeping my nose to the ground."[7] And eight years after this speech, he retains this same image. One of the characters in *Family Voices* (1980) says about another: "She keeps her nose to the grindstone. This I find impressive. There's not too much of that about these days."[8]

Keeping the nose to the ground, to the grindstone, pursuing the image with the greatest vigilance and, once it is found, sticking with it — perhaps these are clues to the weasel and pheasant which are not there, clues to a discovery of the nothing which is precisely meant.

"What am I writing about?" Pinter asked himself in Hamburg, and he answered, "Not the weasel under the cocktail cabinet."[9] What then is the image he pursues with vigor in his plays? Again, he himself gave a clue in a published interview from 1961.

> I start off with people, who come into a particular situation. I certainly don't write from any kind of abstract idea. And I wouldn't know a symbol if I saw one. I don't see that there's anything very strange about *The Caretaker*, for instance, and I can't quite understand why so many people regard it in the way they do. It seems to me a very straightforward and simple play. The germ of my plays? I'll be as accurate as I can about that. I went into a room and saw one person standing up and one person sitting down, and a few weeks later I wrote *The Room*. I went into another room and saw two people sitting down, and a few years later I wrote *The Birthday Party*. I looked through a door into a third room, and saw two people standing up and I wrote *The Caretaker*.[10]

This is, of course, a cryptic clue. But Pinter is consistent. He keeps his nose to this grounding.

So, in a BBC interview with Hallam Tennyson (August 7, 1960), he said,

> Two people in a room — I am dealing a great deal of the time with this image of two people in a room. The curtain goes up on the stage, and I see it as a very potent question: What is going to happen to these two people in the room? Is someone going to open the door and come in?[11]

This is to suggest that something dramatic may occur if the security represented by the room, by the social status quo or by a conventional perspective or by a comfortable and traditional morality is broken and a third factor enters.

Two months after the interview with Hallam Tennyson, Pinter, again on the BBC, was interrogated by Kenneth Tynan. Tynan asked Pinter what his two people in the so-called room are afraid of, to which the author responded,

> Obviously they are scared of what is outside the room. Outside the room there is a world bearing upon them which is frightening.[12]

And then he added, "I am sure it is frightening to you and me as well."[13]

The third factor may be frightening, as frightening as a ghost, but it is that which, for Pinter, makes the drama of drama. So it is this image of the room to which he keeps his nose grounded, this image with which he sticks, from his first play in 1957 until his most recent works.

It all began with dramas of terror and menace, but dramas which were comic nonetheless. *The Room*, written quickly in 1957, opens with Rose and Bert in their flat, their "room." The room "upstairs" has for a long time been vacant; but the "basement" may be stirring with fearful life. There is some indication, during the play, that the room in which Rose and Bert live may be rented right out from under them. In any case, at the end of the play, a "blind Negro" named Riley comes in. He is clearly a threat, especially when he calls Rose by the name of Sal and tells her that her father wants her to come home. Unprovoked, Bert bludgeons the black. Everyone is silent. And Rose utters the final line: "I can't see. I can't see."[14]

In another play from 1957, *The Birthday Party*, Meg and Petey have a room which they rent to Stanley. But then Lulu, who is a "lulu," arrives on the scene, coming between Stanley, the roomer, and Petey's wife, Meg.[15]

*The Dumbwaiter* was also written in 1957, and it, too, has a third dramatic factor, this time, the mechanical contrivance after which the play is named. Ben and Gus, two thugs, are waiting in a basement room, apparently to perform a "hit job." While they are in this underworldly room, the dumbwaiter descends and a voice makes demands "from above" through a speaking tube, demands for gourmet cuisine from all nations, demands that the underworld toughs cannot fulfill. At the end of the play, Ben's revolver is leveled at his buddy Gus for no apparent reason.[16]

A year later in *A Slight Ache*, Edward and Flora confront neither person nor mechanical device. Rather, there is a stinging or biting wasp—they argue over which it is—that comes to their quiet breakfast table. Together, this middle-class couple viciously slays the wasp in a marmalade jar by pouring boiling tea water down the spoonhole in the lid and then squashing the wasp on a plate. But this merely seems to serve to bring on another third, a Matchseller, who is lurking just outside their room, at the back of their house beyond Flora's flower garden. The Matchseller has no dialogue, so in the original radio version it would have been impossible to know for certain whether or not he existed. What is certain is that both Edward and Flora project meanings onto him, this intruder who somehow seems to be a threat. These projections bring to expression the passions of an otherwise blasé twosome. The Matchseller, whose matches are possibly wet and who has, therefore, no fire, becomes the occasion for

Edward and Flora to shift their perspective, finding the "fire" in each other.[17]

And so it goes in Pinter's early plays. In *Night Out* (1959), there are mother and son (Albert), and then there is "the girl," who is a third.[18] In *The Caretaker* (1959), Davies is the third — an "odd one" — in a homosexual triangle with Mick and Aston.[19] And in *The Dwarfs* (1960), Len, who is "crazy," is the irrational third in a relationship with Pete and Mark. All are "dwarfs," and the little people are "powers."[20]

Pinter's triangles moved from cryptic cleverness and theatrical devices of menace, from the black comedy *(Galgenhumor)* of these early plays, to various forms of experimentation during the sixties.

In *The Collection* (1961) the author explores all of the possible dramatic complexities, all of the possible triangles between four persons: a young married couple, Bill and Stella, and a homosexual couple composed of a young man and an old man, James and Harry. The play hints that James may have had an affair with Stella during a business trip. As the play progresses, Bill becomes a friend of James, and Harry visits Stella. And so on. It is as if anyone or any factor can be third to any other twosome.[21]

In the following year, 1962, Pinter wrote *The Lover.* The proper name of the lover, or at least his persona in the play, is Max. But little by little an astonishing fact is revealed to the audience. Max the lover is actually Richard the husband, visiting his own wife, personality transformed, dress radically altered. She, too, is quite changed when her lover Max is with her, profoundly different from the self she manifests in her marriage to Richard. Playacting and/or fantasy . . . this "lover" makes love possible, but "his" nature is that he is a deep and normally unconscious quality of the twosome.

By 1972, the year of *Monologue*, the three are not *The Collection*'s potential complexities of four, nor *The Lover*'s two and the fantasy quality between them. The three, as the title *Monologue* already tells us, are one. The monologue is three fantasies with one voice.[23]

Between *The Lover* and *Monologue* (1962–1972), there appeared from Pinter's pen *Landscape* (1966),[24] *Dialogue for Three* (1964),[25] and *Silence* (1968),[26] in all of which the third factor is a no-thing, a fantasy, an idea. *Tertium non datur* (the third is not given) but it is present all the same in Beth and Duff's *memory* of a Mr. Sykes (*Land-*

*scape*), in "the snow that has turned to slush" (*Dialogue for Three*), and in the *silence* between Runsey and Bates concerning Ellen (*Silence*).

Pinter's experimentation with triangles during the 1960s — all the possible threesomes in four persons, in two persons, and within a single self — led, one might say, to nothing, to no-thing, to "the weasel under the cocktail cabinet": the erotic triangle is in *memoria*; its entanglement is in silence. It is fantasy and a no-thing. This became theatrically explicit in the plays that followed in the seventies, particularly in *Old Times* (1970).[27]

*Old Times* opens with another couple, Deeley and Kate, in their "living room." They are speaking about a third person, Anna, as though she were not present. In fact, she is standing there, in their very room, looking out a window. During the course of the play there is a good deal of talk between Deeley and Anna not only about Anna but also about Kate, talk that suggests that Kate may be dead. And, by the end of the play, there is even a hint that Deeley may have been "done in" earlier than the time of the action of the drama. In all of these suggestions and implications, however, it is mainly Anna who animates the relationship between Deeley and Kate. Anna is alive, even if dead. The third factor is the spirit of the relationship which spirits the relationship, albeit in the fantasy of the couple whose one significant memory is of seeing a movie, perhaps even with Anna, whose title was *Odd Man Out*.

The function of the film in *Old Times* is replaced by a squash game in *Betrayal* eight years later.[28] Again, there is a threesome, a couple, Robert and Emma, and Emma's lover Jerry. Near the middle of the play, Emma wants to watch the two men play squash and after the game, take them to lunch. Her husband Robert, well into his cups, replies:

> Well, to be brutally honest, we wouldn't actually want a woman around, would we, Jerry? I mean a game of squash isn't simply a game of squash, it's rather more than that. You see, first there's the game. And then there's the shower. And then there's the pint. And then there's lunch. After all, you've been at it. You've had your battle. What you want is your pint and your lunch. You really don't want a woman buying you lunch. You don't actually want a woman within a mile of the place, any of the places, really. You don't want her in the squash court, you don't want her in the shower, or the pub, or the restaurant.

You see, at lunch you want to talk about squash, or cricket, or books, or even women, with your friend, and be able to warm to your theme without fear of improper interruption. That's what it's all about.[29]

The eros by triangulation seems to signify the constant refusal to substantialize the third, to keep it in talk, in fantasy, in story; it is not a thing or actual person, but the interplay between two persons (a squash *game* which isn't simply a game of *squash*).

So also, in 1980, in the piece called *Family Voices*, the third factor spoken of between a mother and a son is the dad . . . and he is dead, as he himself tells us! "I have so much to say to you. But I am quite dead. What I have to say to you will never be said."[30]

Now what is going on in all of this?[31] Well, perhaps one might say that in these plays "the weasel under the cocktail cabinet" is the Trinity; and, since the Trinity is ultimately a mystery, under the cabinet of *spiritus* is exactly where it should be. It is not out in the open like three rings on a gas stove, but *under*, in the basement. And the trinitarian form and function of Pinter's plays is all the more fascinating inasmuch as the author shies away from symbolism and overt meanings. They mean, for him, "precisely nothing."

Indeed. The plays move from social dramas of menace and terror in the early years, through experimentations with more subtle triangles in the middle group of plays (triangles that come in fours, in twos, and in the solitary self), to deeper psychological dramaturgy in the most recent works, wherein the triangulations are in dream, fantasy, fictive remembrances, and interior monologues.

It is not that we are attempting to apply trinitarian theology as an interpretive device to Pinter's work; rather, we are trying to view this contemporary drama as itself a secular *theologia*, tales from postmodernity concerning the ultimate, the deepest structures of human consciousness, "the weasel *under* the cocktail cabinet" of our time. What we discover is a Jewish writer, who, quite without authorial intention is intuitively drawn toward a trinitarian form and function which once had manifested itself as a religious "faith seeking understanding," but is now a *theologia* found in a culture. It is secular drama teaching theology to students of religion, rather than students of religion interpreting secular drama theologically.

By attending to this contemporary drama, we can begin to take note of what has become of the Trinity, and what is lacking in the theology of the church and the academy. It is under the cabinet, a menace to be sure, yet alive and well even while, or especially while, hidden. It is as erotic and as mysterious as ever, a true drama of the absurd. *Credo quia absurdum est.* It is, as Pinter's play says, a ghost . . . a Hekatean fact worth attending to in a bit more detail.

In *Old Times*, Deeley sings a line from the popular song "These Foolish Things." The line—"Oh, how the ghost of you clings!"—is familiar and suggestive in the context of the play.[32] This sentiment is expanded upon in a play written four years later, *No Man's Land* (1974), when an old man, Hirst, says to Briggs, who is twenty years his junior:

> I might even show you my photograph album. You might even see a face in it which might remind you of your own, of what you once were. You might see faces of others, in shadow, or cheeks of others, turning, or jaws, or backs of necks, or eyes, dark under hats, which might remind you of others, whom once you knew, whom you thought long dead, but from whom you will still receive a sidelong glance, if you can face the good ghost. Allow the love of the good ghost.[33]

But why should Briggs look the ghost in the face? Why should he embrace the ghostly and the ghastly? Hirst explains.

> They possess all that emotion . . . trapped. Bow to it. It will assuredly never release them, but who knows . . . what relief . . . it may give to them . . . who knows how they may quicken . . . in their chains, in their glass jars. You think it cruel . . . to quicken them, when they are fixed, imprisoned? No . . . no. Deeply, deeply, they wish to respond to your touch, to your look, and when you smile, their joy . . . is unbounded. And so I say to you, tender the dead, as you would yourself be tendered, now, in what you would describe as your life.[34]

The ghost gives emotion, deep feeling. It gives, by way of memory's love, life. So, we should "tender the dead," allowing "the love of the good ghost," according to Pinter's Hirst.

But there is an additional oddness in the function of the ghost, additional to the paradox that that which is dead gives life. For when Briggs looks into the photograph album where he may see himself and his life, he says, "They're blank, mate, blank. The blank dead." "Nonsense," Hirst responds.[35] It is somehow reminiscent of the Fool speaking to Lear: "Can you make no use of nothing, Nuncle?"[36]

Pinter stays with the ghostly image. In *Old Times* Kate says, "You talk of me as if I were dead." And Anna says, "No, no, you weren't dead, you were so lively, so animated, you used to laugh—." Kate replies, "I said you talk about me as if I *am* dead. Now."[37] Similarly, in *Monologue* the voice of a man says:

> You often, I'll be frank, act as if you're dead, as if the Balls Pond Road, and the lovely ebony lady never existed, as if the rain in the light on the pavements in the twilight never existed, as if our sporting and intellectual life never was.[38]

Yet, the story of love, of eros, does still exist in the man's memory and in the fantasy of that memory, even though "sometimes I think you've forgotten the black girl, the ebony one,"[39] just as sometimes it would seem that the Trinity, the third, the ghost, is neither tendered nor loved in our tradition. As Pinter has written in *The Dwarfs*, "giving up the ghost isn't so much a failure as a tactical error,"[40] a theological error that students of religion apparently have made, but one that is made by neither Pinter nor his drama, with its secularized trinitarian insightfulness.

The insight in Pinter's plays has to do with the self. In the interview with Kenneth Tynan, Pinter said:

> I'm dealing with these characters at the extreme edge of their living, where they are living pretty much alone, at their hearth, their home hearth. . . . We all, I think . . . may have sexual relationships or go to political meetings or discuss ideas, but when we get back to our rooms and we are faced with a bed and we are either alone or with someone else, then . . . I don't think we go on long about ideas of political allegiances. . . . I mean, there comes a point, surely, where this living in *the* world must be tied up with living in *your* own world, where you are—in your room.[41]

The room in Pinter's plays is the self that contains two personae, and into which comes a third, making for the "drama" of the drama. This is perhaps most plainly put in a speech by Len in *The Dwarfs*.

> The point is, who are you? Not why or how, not even what. I can see what, perhaps, clearly enough. But who are you? It's no use saying you know who you are just because you tell me you can fit your particular key into a particular slot, which will only receive your particular key, because that's not foolproof and certainly not conclusive. Just because you're inclined to make these statements of faith has nothing to do with me. It's not my business. Occasionally I believe I perceive a little of what you are but that's pure accident. Pure accident on both our parts,

the perceived and the perceiver. It's nothing like an accident, it's deliberate, it's a joint pretense. We depend on these accidents, on these contrived accidents, to continue. It's not important then that it's conspiracy or hallucination. What you are, or appear to be to me, or appear to be to you, changes so quickly, so horrifyingly, I certainly can't keep up with it and I'm damn sure you can't either. But who you are I can't even begin to recognize, and sometimes I recognize it so wholly, so forcibly, I can't look, and how can I be certain of what I see?[42]

Then Len makes the point, in response to his own question about the self, a point about the ghastliness of ghosts which cling.

You're the sum of so many reflections. How many reflections? Whose reflections? Is that what you consist of? What scum does the tide leave?[43]

The church fathers might have asked, What coagulation (*hypostasis*) is left in the tracings of the unknown and unknowable God? What *vestigia trinitatis?* Len goes on speaking about the unknown and unknowable self.

What happens to the scum? When does it happen? I've seen what happens. But I can't speak when I see it. I can only point a finger. I can't even do that. The scum is broken and sucked back. I don't see where it goes. I don't see when, what do I see, what have I seen? What have I seen, the scum or the essence? . . .[44]

the *hypostasis* or the *ousia,* the personae or the "substance" of the Trinity? Len says:

What about it? Does all this give you the right to stand there and tell me you know who you are? It's a bloody impertinence. . . .[45]

just as it is a theological impertinence to speak about the mystery of the Trinity.

But it is a "bloody impertinence" *not* to speak of it, also. As Samuel Beckett said, "Nothing to say, no way to say it, together with an obligation to speak" (*Molloy. Malone Dies. The Unnamable* [London: Calder, 1959], 28, 316). So, Pinter has spoken with precision about the nothing, embodying in his drama a trinitarian perspective.

To be sure, the tradition has for a long time spoken about the self as tripartite (body, soul, spirit), just as it has spoken about God as a Trinity. Yet, the psychological tradition, until the depth psychology of Freud and Jung (see part 1, interlude), often neglected the third —

the ebony lady, the ghost, the no-thing, fantasy, the un-conscious; in this way the psychological tradition has been not unlike the theological tradition, which has focused most of its attention on the Father and the Son, not knowing quite what to do with the Ghost, the Spirit. The third has been a menacing factor, as Joachim of Fiore and Montanus discovered in their dealings with orthodoxy.

Boethius defined the self as "individual substance of a rational nature,"[46] thereby accounting for body and spirit/mind, but leaving out soul. But on the other hand, there have been pentecostal attempts to substantialize the third, committing *spiritual* idolatry, and thereby losing spirit in the name of "spirit." In Pinter's drama, however, we are once again nudged into, as St. Paul says, "speaking of spiritual things in a spiritual manner."[47] In the work of this postmodern playwright, the third is present by virtue of its absence, and it is absent when objectivized in the present.

Nor should this contemporary dramatic perspective have been surprising. It is in form and matter very like the arguments of St. Augustine which were reviewed in chapter 2. All of the theological motifs are in place: the correspondence between the structures of self and the drama of the triune life of the godhead; amor as the connecting factor, the third, which is always a mystery; the mystery as spiritual finally seen only "in a glass darkly," the glass being the transparent self and the darkness being the *vestigia*, the tracings of the transpersonal in the personal. For finally, in Augustine as in Pinter, the Trinity is invisible, like "the weasel under the cocktail cabinet," indicating precisely a no-thing which is the nature of self as much as it is the nature of God, a "counterpointed trio of memory."[48] Pinter tropes Augustine in our day, and Augustine's *De Trinitate* provides a troping of a postmodern drama which means "precisely nothing."

We need such tropings, such transformations by way of poetic metaphor. Northrop Frye has recently explained why.

> The sense in Christianity of a faith beyond reason . . . is closely connected with the linguistic fact that many of the central doctrines of traditional Christianity can be grammatically expressed only in the form of metaphor. Thus: Christ is God and man; in the Trinity three persons *are* one; in the Real Presence the body and blood *are* the bread and the wine. When these doctrines are rationalized by conceptions of a spiritual substance and the like, the metaphor is tranlated into meto-

nymic language and "explained." But there is a strong smell of intellectual morality about such explanations, and sooner or later they fade away and the original metaphor reappears, as intransigent as ever. At that point we are back to a world in which St. Patrick illustrates the doctrine of the Trinity by a shamrock, a use of concrete paradox that enlightens the mind by paralyzing the discursive reason, like the koan of Zen Buddhism. The doctrines . . . can be stated only in a metaphorical this-is-that form.[49]

So it has been. The Trinity has been a powerful metaphor. Attempts at theo*logical* explanation murdered the notion by not recognizing it to be metaphorical at base. But there comes a time in the history of the race, as in the history of individuals, when the repressed return. The trinitarian insight, in its metaphorical mode, resurfaced not only in Freud and Jung (part 1, interlude), not only in philosophy, the social sciences, and literary criticism (part 2, interlude), but also — and perhaps, because of the "ghost," most radically — in the theopoetic drama of Harold Pinter. If his theater of the absurd seems a bit Zennish, so much the better for theology today, as well as for our culture's drama. It then more resembles the shamrock of St. Patrick and the rose of Jabès.

# 6

## THE BODY OF GOD
## God Who Is a Trinity
## Is Love Which Is Triangular

The poets, novelists, and dramatists have much to teach theology. Their works suggest a poetic and dramatic perspective on the Trinity, bringing concrete image and feeling to a theological idea. And the theopoetic of these contemporary artists, with its dramatic sense, demonstrates in image and action that the Trinity may itself be a perspective on the theater of everyday life-experience.

In the religious consciousness of the West, the Trinity conventionally has been thought to be a belief about ultimate reality, about God. It is also and ultimately, however, a divine perspective on life. The trinitarian perspective, in the face of disbelief as well as belief, aims at a different dimension, a dimension of otherness, a dimension of depth. Thus, a truly trinitarian theology will be a "depth theology"— a theologizing (remembering, contemplating, and loving) that emerges out of the depths of life, ministers to the deepest of life's experiences, and constantly returns to the depth of signification. As St. Paul wrote, "God has revealed to us through the Spirit; for the Spirit searches everything, even the depths of God" (1 Cor. 2:10, RSV).

God who is the Trinity is not merely an object of belief. That God is dead for many who have experienced the most profound depths. But — *mirabile dictu!* — precisely in such depth experience, which may be seen as the "depths of God," the Trinity is re-visioned as vision, reborn as perspective. Something similar to this drama had happened to Nicholas of Cusa some five centuries before Harold Pinter brought it to our attention again.

The mystical Cusanus served the church not without deep and

bitter struggle with his religion and with the church's institutional forms. He was vicar general, bishop, and cardinal. In June of 1452, when fifty-one years old, he spent two happy days at the reformed Benedictine Abbey of Tegernsee. The monks there were instructed in Cusanus's version of the Neoplatonic idea of *coincidentia oppositorum* (the coincidence of opposites) in a third which is not given, *tertium non datur*. He linked to this notion the Augustinian teaching concerning the *doctra ignorantia* (the learned ignorance).

The teaching awoke in the monks what the prior, Bernard de Waging, called "new longings." So much was this the case that Nicholas was begged to return and give further instruction in the contemplative life. His response came in December of the following year. At that time he sent his friends a little manual of meditation entitled *De visione Dei* (The vision of God) in which the metaphor of being up against a "wall" was used to help the monks experience the meaning of the Trinity.

Nicholas himself had come to this experience by a difficult path. In a letter to Cardinal Guiliano Cesarini, he recalled a crucial moment during a boat trip from Greece to Italy in November of 1437. Cusanus wrote,

> Now receive what I have long sought by different paths, but found only while I was on shipboard returning from Greece; . . . I was led to conceive the incomprehensible in an incomprehensible way in the knowledge of non-knowledge.[1]

About this shipboard insight, Karl Jaspers has said, "This was not just one more idea, it was a new kind of thinking. It carried . . . a new dimension of depth."[2]

This "new kind of thinking"—a depth theology—was the way in which Nicholas instructed his monk-friends. It began by acknowledging that the religious quest is, in its most radical form, a quest for a God who remains forever hidden from our human abilities to grasp.[3] For example, the doctrine of the Trinity—the instance of conceiving God to be a One that is Three or a Threesome who are One, Infinite yet everything Finite—has the intentional function, not unlike a Zen koan or the theater of the absurd, of frustrating arrogant and idolatrous human knowing. In religion we come up against "the wall of absurdity" and understanding "seems as if impossible."[4] "The wall is a barrier," he wrote, "to the power of every intellect,"[5] including, especially, the intellect of a believer. This is, of course, reminiscent of St. Augustine's saying, "Who can understand the omnipotent Trinity? And yet who does not speak about it, if indeed it is of it that he speaks? Rare is the soul who, when he speaks of it, also knows of what he speaks."[6]

This humbling of certitude in theology and of every religious literalism led Nicholas prayerfully to warn, "If anyone should set forth any concept by which Thou couldst be conceived, I know that that concept is not a concept of Thee, for every concept is ended in the wall."[7] So, the sense of religious depth lies precisely in the experience of limit and limitation; religious depth goes hand in hand with being in the depths, with not-knowing, with knowing precisely nothing, being up against the wall.

Since this radical experience is the locus of a deep sense of things, Nicholas could advise that "it behoveth . . . the intellect to become ignorant and to abide in darkness, if it would fain see thee. But what, O my God," he implored, "is this intellectual ignorance?" And then he answered: "Is it not an instructed ignorance? For Thou, O God, who art infinity, canst only be approached by him whose intellect is in ignorance, to wit, by him who knows himself to be ignorant of Thee."[8]

Therefore, Cusanus continued, "How needful it is . . . to enter into the darkness, and to admit the coincidence of opposites beyond all reason. . . . For thou canst not be seen elsewhere than where impossibility meeteth and faceth me."[9]

It would seem that human darkness, being up against it, in the depths, is somehow a theological advantage, as if experience of the absence of God is not far from the presence of the godhead which is not some-*thing* but is a no-thing. When we are in the dark, at soul's limit, where attempts to reason and to sense something are up against a wall, a new way of thinking and speaking may emerge, a radically different way, a way which has a depth dimension to it. Certainly, with the erotic mystery of the Trinity of God (not to mention the triangles of self, mind, and sense) we are up against the wall.

But between mind and sense, between intelligibles and sensibles, there is image and imagination (see the introduction). When we are up against the wall, in the depths, images come. We imagine things which, of course, are not things at all, being imaginal as such visions are. So, the poet Rilke wrote:

> You, neighbor God, if sometimes in the night
> I rouse you with loud knocking, I do so
> only because I seldom hear you breathe;
> I know: you are alone.
> And should you need a drink, no one is there
> to reach it to you, groping in the dark.
> Always I hearken. Give but a small sign.
> I am quite near . . .[10]

suggesting that we are near to God when it is night and we are groping in the dark, which, in the case of this poem, is the darkness of God, the depths of God. Yet, the poem continues . . .

> Between us there is but a narrow wall,
> and by sheer chance; for it would take
> merely a call from your lips or from mine
> to break it down,
> and that without a sound.
> The wall is built of your images.[11]

Not only are our images idols (our sensations and our conceptions which block the way to the no-thing by imagining it to be a some-thing), but our images also, when up against the wall, can be icons, ways of imaging what we seek, traces, *vestigia trinitatis*.

Following the Augustinian clue in this book, we have attempted to "keep our nose to this ground" ("there not being much of that around these days" in theology as in drama), trying to stay with the *vestigia*, the images of psychological eros, in the person (part 1), in thinking (part 2), and in the drama of consciousness itself (part 3). For images and imagination give body to things unknown and unknowable.

It all seems to have to do with the Holy Ghost and imagination. Indeed, as we have explored the mythos of the Christian *doctrine* of the Trinity—probing it backwards into likeness between theological idea and psychological image and downwards into Greek myths of Zeus and Hera, ghosted by Hekate, following this pagan sense into Neoplatonic and alchemical theologizing, noting a re-visioned image of *persona* as face and *hypostasis* as coagulation, and then leading the imaginal complex of Trinity forward in time by way of poets, novelists, and dramatists—at every turn the suggestion and implication has been in the direction of image as ghost and ghost as image.

The astonishing matter is, however, that the imagined ghost and the ghostly imagination function not to spiritualize, as abstract ideas seem to do, but rather to give body to spiritual ideas. Ideas, like relationships, often need body. From time to time they need coagulation, some face that we can face. And this is what the Trinity offers: the image of a God, who is love, which is ultimately triangular, giving body.

Is it not the case that when we are in love, images come? We are up against it, not knowing how to sense it or think about it. Our life-plots thicken and coagulate. Life gets sticky, viscous, sweet as honey, fiery like sulfur, full of savor as salt, bitter as gall. Love is triangular, and triangles are not easy. But they function to bring fantasy and imagination to life, fantasies and imaginings that embody what we know neither how to sense nor how to think about.

The Trinity is an image of love, and as an image of God who is love, it is at once the poetry of God (theopoetic) and the body of God. God, who is a Trinity, is love, which is—whether we sense it or not, whether we know it or not—triangular. When we are up against the wall, in religion or in love, the Trinity is the image of our situation. Our deepest, if darkest, moments are our allies.

If the poet Rilke worried about this "wall," Nicholas of Cusa took advantage of it. It is our ignorance, even our learned ignorance (*docta ignorantia*), and it is by such ignorance, caught in the oppositions of life and knowing, that we are led to a theological imagination that he calls *coincidentia oppositorum*.

In December of 1453, along with the manual on how to experience the Trinity, Nicholas sent a Hekatean picture of Jesus to the monks. It was one of those pictures in which the eyes seem to look at you no matter where you are standing in the room. Nicholas told the monks to put this face up on the wall and then to watch it looking at each of them individually. The eyes looked at each of them at the same time, no matter where each was standing. They were experiencing a paradox. It was as if the center of the wall, where the picture was, were simultaneously in touch with each point on the circumference of the semicircle of monks who surrounded it.

Then Nicholas told the monks to contemplate their situation. He asked them to notice that the vision and the visioning, their seeing a picture which was seeing them, were not coming from "the other side" of the wall. Rather, the visioning came precisely from the wall — the wall which one might have thought to be a mere barrier between self and "other." With this particular image on the wall, the experience of the wall took on new perspective.

So, Nicholas wrote; "I see Thee, good Jesu, within the wall," not beyond it. And then he added; "Within the wall of Paradise . . . truth and image are alike." "Love is a treasure," he wrote, "secret and hidden, since 'tis found within the wall of the coincident of hidden and manifest. . . . I am lover, I am loveable, and I am the bond between."[12]

So it was that every monk facing the wall, which was a face of the trinitarian mystery, saw himself being seen in trinitarian perspective. As this mystery dawned, the seeker might have noted: My face is the only face I have. And it is not mine. It is God's Face, the face I had before I was born. A good ghost. Experienced by way of love's coagulations.

In this trinitarian perspective, it is humankind, triangled erotically, that is the coagulation of God, when up against it, filled with images and imaginings, deeply ghosted while allowing the love of "the ebony lady," or whatever third there may be. For Hekate is many-headed, like the Trinity; and, like Nicholas's image of Christ, her ghost is many-eyed, so richly faceted as to be guardian angel for each and all, and for each and every dimension of the deepest self, leading through the valley of the shadow of depth . . . perhaps to new heights, but new heights always within the depth of imagination's sense.

Perhaps it was, therefore, the Trinity which was secreted in the imagination that touched Henry David Thoreau, when, in his *Journals,* he wrote:

> I just looked up at a fine twinkling star and thought that a voyager whom I know, now many days' sail from this coast, might possibly be looking up at that same star with me. The stars are the apexes of what triangles![13]

It is a very important question. What triangles, indeed?

# NOTES

## INTRODUCTION
## THEOLOGY
## AS REMEMBERING,
## CONTEMPLATING, AND LOVING

1. Augustine, *The Confessions*, XIII.11, trans. A. C. Outler (Philadelphia: Westminster Press, 1955); cf. Augustine, *De Trinitate*, I.1; V.8; X.2; XV.8–10, 27, 28.

2. The former of these corresponds somewhat to the Platonic method, and also to idealism generally; the latter, to Aristotelianism, and also to empiricism and utilitarianism. Paul Tillich has discussed something similar to this typology in "The Two Types of Philosophy of Religion," *Theology of Culture*, ed. R. C. Kimball (New York: Oxford University Press, 1959), 10–29.

3. C. G. Jung, *Memories, Dreams, Reflections* (New York: Pantheon Books, 1963), 141f. Cf. *Collected Works*, 20 vols., (Princeton: Princeton University Press, 1953–1979), IX.i.34–38. (Hereafter cited as *CW*.)

4. Sigmund Freud, *Introductory Lectures on Psychoanalysis*, trans. J. Strachey (New York: W. W. Norton, 1966), 19.

5. Clement of Alexandria, *Paidagogus*, III.1. Cf. Hippolytus, *Elenchos*, X.34.4: "For to him who knows himself it is given to be known of him by whom he is called." Olympiodorus, citing Zosimos, says, "When thou knowest thyself, thou knowest also the God who is truly one." Cited by Jung, *CW* XIII.372.

6. Cf. the use of the word "depth" in the theology of Paul Tillich, "Two Types," 7; and *Systematic Theology*, vol. 3 (Chicago: University of Chicago Press, 1963), 113. See Abraham Heschel, "Depth Theology," *The Insecurity of Freedom* (New York: Farrar, Straus, and Giroux, 1966), 115–26.

7. Jung, *CW*, XVIII.1164.

8. Ibid., XIII.555.

9. Ibid., XIII.75.

10. Ibid., IX.i.22.

11. Cf. Joseph Campbell, *The Flight of the Wild Gander* (New York: Viking Press, 1969), 33: "Mythology is psychology misread as cosmology, history, and biography."

12. This *mundus imaginalis*, a third way between intelligibles and sensibles, has been charted at length by Henry Corbin. See *"Mundus Imaginalis, or The Imaginary and the Imaginal" Spring 1972;* "Pour une charte de l'Imaginal," *Corps spirituel et Terre celeste* (Paris: Editions Buchet/Chastel, 1979), 7–19; and, *Creative Imagination in the Sufism of Ibn 'Abrabi,* trans. R. Manheim (London: Routledge and Kegan Paul, 1970), 240. Cf. James Hillman, *Dream and the Underworld* (New York: Harper & Row, 1979), 1–6.

13. Augustine uses the term *ideae principales,* rather than *archetypos* in *De diversis quaestionibus,* LXXXIII. Jung acknowledges his source in Augustine in *CW,* VIII.275; IX.i.5; and XI.845.

14. Augustine, *De Trinitate,* XIV.2.

15. What this introduction attempts to articulate for the study of theology also has been proposed by James Hillman for a study of mythology. See Hillman's *The Myth of Analysis* (Evanston: Northwestern University Press, 1972), 196: "Mythology's moments of anxiety, bestiality, and possession, its extraordinary nonhuman imaginal happenings, can be newly illumined through our own corresponding experiences. Mythology can then reach us, and we it, in a fresh way because it bears directly on our pain. More: our pain becomes a way of gaining insight into mythology. We enter a myth and take part in it directly through our afflictions. The fantasies that emerge from our complexes become the gate into mythology."

16. *The Freud/Jung Letters,* ed. W. McGuire (Princeton: Princeton University Press, 1974), 294.

17. Justin Martyr, *Apology,* I.21–22. In more recent days, Heinz Westman has demonstrated the psychological vitality of religious and mythological images. See Westman, *The Springs of Creativity* (New York: Atheneum, 1961), and *The Structure of Biblical Myths* (Dallas: Spring Publications, 1984).

18. Aristotle, *Metaphysics,* Lambda i.1074a38–b14; Beta 4.1000b9–19. Cf. D. L. Miller, *The New Polytheism* (Dallas: Spring Publications, 1981), chaps. 1 and 3.

19. Cf. James Hillman, "An Inquiry into Image," *Spring 1977* (Dallas: Spring Publications, 1977), 62–88; "Further Notes on Images," *Spring 1978* (Dallas: Spring Publications, 1978), 152–82; and, "Image Sense," *Spring 1979* (Dallas: Spring Publications, 1979), 130–43.

20. Origen, *Peri archōn* ("On First Principles"), III.vi.1, trans. G. W. Butterworth (New York: Harper & Row, 1966). Cf. Origen, *Contra Celsum,* IV.30; Irenaeus, *Adv. haer.* ("Against the Heresies"), V.6; and Clement of Alexandria, *Stromata* ("Miscellanies"), II.38.5.

21. Rainer Maria Rilke, *Duino Elegies,* trans. J. Leishman and S. Spender (New York: W. W. Norton, 1939), 85.

22. Wallace Stevens, "The Owl in the Sarcophagus," *The Collected Poems* (New York: Alfred A. Knopf, 1975), 433.

23. Stanley Romaine Hopper is preeminently the one who has shown the way in our time to a poetic theology, which he calls theo*poetic* as opposed to the*ology* . As I do in this introduction, Hopper speaks of three moments. He calls them the step back, the step down, and the step through. See "Le cri de Merlin," *Anagogic Qualities of Literature*, ed. J. Strelka (University Park: Pennsylvania State University Press, 1971), 9–35; "Symbolic Reality and the Poet's Task," *Eranos 34–1975* (Zurich: Rhein Verlag, 1967), 167–218; "Jerusalem's Wall and Other Perimeters," *Humanities, Religion, and the Arts Tomorrow*, ed. H. Hunter (New York: Holt, Rinehart, & Winston, 1972), 228–45. Cf. Amos Wilder, *Theopoetic* (Philadelphia: Fortress Press, 1976), in which there is a discussion of Hopper's work, specifically, and the relation of religion to the imaginal domain, generally.

24. Rilke, *Duino Elegies*, 85.

25. James Joyce, *Finnegans Wake* (New York: Viking Press, 1939), 304 n.

1

IMAGES AND FANTASIES HIDDEN<br>IN RELIGIOUS TRADITIONS

1. Nicholas Berdyaev, *Christian Existentialism*, trans. W. Lowrie (New York: Harper & Row, 1965), 53. The citation is from Berdyaev's work, *Freedom and the Spirit*, vol. 2, (1927–28), 20.

2. Paul Tillich, *Systematic Theology*, vol. 3 (Chicago: University of Chicago Press, 1963), 293.

3. Jacob Boehme, *Six Theosophic Points*, I.21, trans. J. R. Earle (Ann Arbor: University of Michigan Press, 1958).

4. Franz Pfeifer, *Meister Eckhart*, trans. C. de B. Evans (London: John M. Watkins, 1924), Tract. XI.

5. Augustine, *City of God*, X.24, 26, 28, trans. H. Bettenson (Baltimore: Penguin Books, 1972). Cf. *De Trinitate*, VIII.7–10; IX.2–3; X.8; XIV.2, 14; XV.11.

6. Raymond Pannikar, *The Trinity and World Religions* (Madras: The Christian Literary Society, 1970).

7. Georges Dumézil, *Archaic Roman Religion*, 2 vols., trans. P. Krapp (Chicago: University of Chicago Press, 1966).

8. Gerardus Van der Leeuw, *Religion in Essence and Manifestation*, vol. 1, trans. J. E. Turner (New York: Harper & Row, 1963), xix.2 (170).

9. Philip Wheelwright, *The Burning Fountain: A Study of the Language of Symbolism* (Bloomington: Indiana University Press, 1968), 132–35. See also the remarkable demonstration of the truly ancient and archetypal nature of the trinitarian notion (neolithic period!) in Heinz Westman, *The Structure of Biblical Myths: The Ontogenesis of the Psyche* (Dallas: Spring Publications, 1983), 71–77.

10. Frank Reynolds, "The Several Bodies of Buddha: Reflections on a Neglected Aspect of Theravada Tradition," *History of Religions* 16.4 (1977):

374–89. See John Strong, "The Transforming Gift: An Analysis of Devotional Acts of Offering in Buddhist *Avadāna* Literature," *History of Religions* 18.3 (1979): 226. I am completely indebted to my colleague, Professor Richard Pilgrim, for this data on Buddhism. See his "Six Circles, One Dewdrop: The Religio-Aesthetic of Komparu Zenchiku," *Chanoyu Quarterly* 33 (1983): 7–23. See also Nagao Gadjin, "On the Theory of the Buddha-Body," *Eastern Buddhist*, n.s. VI.1 (1973), 25–53.

11. W. L. Dulière, *De la dyade à l'unité par la triade* (Paris: Adrien Maisonneuve, 1965), passim. As one examines the pictures which are reproduced on the following pages, it may be not beside the point to compare their ancient artistry with the words of a contemporary painter, Stephen De Staebler. In a conversation with Diane Apostolos-Cappadona, De Staebler was reflecting upon the difficulty a painter or sculptor has in "dealing with the male-female polarity and the form of the body." His interlocutor observed that in his art De Staebler is "striving for harmonious oneness." The artist responded: "It is one of the great quests of being human, even though we are so involved with the polarity of man and woman. I do not know what to make of the Trinity. I keep thinking about it, as I see the Holy Spirit as the vehicle for the fusion of opposites. It is the force that allows us to transcend our separateness. Without the Holy Spirit, we are caught in an almost frozen separation. It is like the water that allows the fish to swim. It allows fusion or unity to occur through the force of love; it bridges the gulf between parties who do love each other. The Bible is full of the problem of separation, like the prodigal son: the conflict between people who essentially love each other, but hate is there also." (Diane Apostolos-Cappadona, ed., *Art, Creativity, and the Sacred* [New York: Crossroad, 1984], 29f.)

12. Zenkei Shibyama, *Zen Comments on the Mumonkan*, trans. S. Kudo (New York: New American Library, 1974), 132.

13. Ibid., 133.

14. Ibid., 134.

15. Ibid., 135.

16. Zenkei Shibyama, *A Flower Does Not Talk*, trans. S. Kudo (Rutland, Vt.: Charles Tuttle, 1971), 244, 245.

17. Augustine, *The Confessions*, XIII.11.

18. Virgil, *Eclogue*, VIII.76, trans. G. Lee (Baltimore: Penguin Books, 1980).

19. Marsilio Ficino, *Commentary on Plato's Symposium on Love*, II.1, trans. S. Jayne (Dallas: Spring Publications, 1985).

20. Tertullian, *Adv. Prax.*, II (cited in Paul Tillich, *A History of Christian Thought*, ed. C. E. Braaten [New York: Harper & Row, 1968], 46); cf. J. N. Kelly, *Early Christian Doctrines* (New York: Harper & Row, 1978), 110ff; Eberhard Jungel, *The Doctrine of the Trinity: God's Being Is in His Becoming* (Grand Rapids: Eerdmans, 1976); Jürgen Moltmann, *The Trinity and the Kingdom: The Doctrine of God* (New York: Harper & Row, 1981). For a study of the biblical basis of the trinitarian idea, along with its triadic source

in Jewish tradition and Scripture, see Jane Schaberg, *The Father, the Son and the Holy Spirit* (Chico: Scholars Press, 1982).

21. Cf. Kelly, *Early Christian Doctrines*, 129.

22. Augustine, *De Trinitate*, V.8; cf. VII.4.

23. Cited in Jung, *CW*, XI.218.

24. E. R. Hardy and C. C. Richardson, eds., *Christology of the Later Fathers* (Philadelphia: Westminster Press, 1954), 378f.

25. Augustine, *Confessions*, XIII.22.

26. Ibid.

27. Augustine, *Enchiridion*, XII.38, trans. A. C. Outler (Philadelphia: Westminster Press, 1955).

28. See Tillich, *A History of Christian Thought*, 117. Augustine also says "When it [*i.e.*, the mind in its knowledge of itself] is turned upon itself . . . a trinity occurs [*e.g.*, a word in *thought*, joined to *memory*, by *will*]." Cited in Frederick Goldin, *The Mirror of Narcissus in the Courtly Love Lyric* (Ithaca: Cornell University Press, 1967), 44.

29. Jacob Boehme, *Six Theosophic Points*, I.21.

30. Augustine, *Of True Religion*, XXXIX.72, trans. J. H. S. Burleigh (Chicago: Henry Regnery, 1959).

31. Augustine, *Confessions*, X.27. Cf. *De Trinitate*, X.2–3, 8; XIII.2; XIV.2, 14; XV.9; and Origen, *On First Principles*, IV.iv.5: "Every rational creature needs to participate in the Trinity."

## INTERLUDE
### FREUD AND JUNG

1. Norman O. Brown, *Love's Body* (New York: Random House, 1966), 60.

2. Sigmund Freud, *On Creativity and the Unconscious*, ed. B. Nelson (New York: Harper & Row, 1958), 65f.

3. Ibid., 66.

4. Ibid.

5. Christine Downing, *The Goddess: Mythological Images of the Feminine* (New York: Crossroad, 1981), 85.

6. Ibid.

7. Sigmund Freud, *The Origins of Psychoanalysis: Letters to Wilhelm Fliess*, trans. E. Mosbacher and J. Strachey (New York: Basic Books, 1954), 215ff.

8. Sigmund Freud, *Introductory Lectures on Psychoanalysis*, trans. J. Strachey (New York: W. W. Norton, 1966), 368.

9. Ibid., 371.

10. See Eric Berne, *Games People Play: The Psychology of Human Relationships* (New York: Grove Press, 1964); and, *What Do You Say After Hello?* (New York: Bantam Books, 1973).

11. Stephen Karpman, "Fairy Tales and Script Drama Analysis," *Transactional Analysis Bulletin* 7 (April 1968): 39–43. Cf. Berne, *What Do You Say*

*After Hello?,* 186ff.

12. Berne, *What Do You Say After Hello?,* 187.

13. See Norman O. Brown, *Life Against Death* (New York: Vintage, 1959), chap. 7, and passim.

14. Ibid.

15. Jung, "Answer to Job," *CW,* XI, prefatory note, 358.

16. Plato, *Timaeus,* 31B–C, trans. B. Jowett in *The Collected Dialogues of Plato,* ed. E. Hamilton and H. Cairns (Princeton: Princeton University Press, 1961): "Two things alone cannot properly be conjoined without a third; for there must be some bond between them tying them together." Cf. Proclus, *Commentary on Timaeus,* LXXXIII.265.

17. Jung, "Zur Psychologie der Trinitätsidee," *Eranos 8–1940–41,* 36, 45, 47. But compare this with *CW,* IX.i.267: "An archetypal content expresses itself, first and foremost, in metaphors. If such a content should speak of the sun and identify it with a lion, the king, the hoard of gold guarded by the dragon, or the power that makes for the life and health of man, it is neither the one thing nor the other, but the unknown third thing that finds more or less adequate expression in all these similes, yet — to the perpetual vexation of the intellect — remains unknown and not to be fitted into a formula."

18. Jung, "Zur Psychologie der Trinitätsidee," 50.

19. Ibid., 46. On p. 48 Jung quotes the theologian Kopgen as saying, "Trinity is not only a revelation of God but also of man."

20. Ibid., 64.

21. In the 1948 published version of the essay on the Trinity, Jung indicated how pressing this matter was when he stated that he felt under a kind of "moral obligation to return to this theme" (*CW,* XI.169). In fact, he kept returning to it, or perhaps it to him, during his entire life.

22. Jung, *Letters,* vol. 1 (Princeton: Princeton University Press, 1972), 300.

23. Ibid., vol. 1, 391.

24. Ibid., vol. 1, 449.

25. See Jung, *CW,* VII.119; VII.413; IX.i.12–17; X.643; XI.474–87; XVI.378 n. 30.

26. Jung, *Memories, Dreams, Reflections,* 13ff.

27. Jung, *Letters,* vol. 2, 377.

28. Cf. Jung, "If Christ Walked the Earth Today," *CW,* XVIII.1461.

29. Jung, *CW,* IV.106; V.198; etc.

30. Ibid., IX.i.425–31; XI.245ff; XII.192, 333; etc.

31. Ibid., IX.ii.156; XII.228; XIV.122 n. 52, 355, 643; etc.

32. Ibid., XIV.68 n. 170.

33. Ibid., XIII.474.

34. Ibid., XI.218.

35. Ibid., XI.170. Cf. Jung's saying: "What depths in the soul were stirred by that great turning point in human history [*i.e.,* trinitarian thinking]." (*CW,* XI.242).

36. Edward Edinger, *Ego and Archetype* (Baltimore: Penguin Books, 1973), 179–94. This chapter was originally a lecture at the Second International Conference for Analytical Psychology in Zurich, 1972.

37. John Layard, "The Third Uniting Factor," *Journal of Analytical Psychology* 11.1 (1966): 41ff.

38. Wolfgang Geigerich, "On the Neurosis of Psychology or the Third of the Two," *Spring 1977* (Zurich: Spring Publications, 1977), 153ff.

39. Russell Lockhart, "Eros in Language, Myth, and Dream," *Quadrant* (Summer 1978): 57–59.

40. Raphael Lopez-Pedraza, *Hermes and His Children* (Dallas: Spring Publications, 1977), 62ff, 76–79. Lopez writes: "Although a psychology of the trio seems to be beyond the scope of basic training in psychotherapy, our aim is to see trio psychology as a basic constellation in psychotherapy. This cannot be taught or learned in terms of training, only life itself with the help of Hermes might provide the possibilities for perceiving and insighting the formation of trio images in psychotherapy. We psychologists have to take into account that the analytical psychotherapeutical eros involves, more often than we think (or probably always), a third person, and this third one makes us doubtful about the temenos of only analyst and patient. In reality, either hidden or apparent, there is invariably a third" (p. 64).

41. James Hillman, "Schism," *Loose Ends* (Dallas: Spring Publications, 1975), 89ff; *The Myth of Analysis* (Evanston: Northwestern University Press, 1972), 97ff; and, *Inter Views* (New York: Harper & Row, 1983), 186f.

42. Hillman, "Schism," 89f.

43. Hillman, *Myth of Analysis*, 97.

44. Ibid.

45. Ibid., 97f. Cf. Hillman's statement in *Inter Views:* "I meant love that is fixated to pairing, coupling, the dyad, the delusion of reciprocity. . . . A third has to come in. Love itself makes this move. It brings in the triangle, and that's the importance of jealousy: it makes you awfully conscious of the third. . . . Imagination is the thing, and love cannot happen without the third" (p. 186).

46. See n. 8.

47. Søren Kiekegaard, *Fear and Trembling/Sickness unto Death*, trans. W. Lowrie (Garden City: Doubleday, 1955), 146f.


2

LIFE-LIKENESS AND UNLIKENESS

1. *The Gospel of Thomas*, logion 5.

2. Gen. 1:26; 1 Cor. 13:12.

3. Augustine, *De Trinitate*, XV.20, trans. A. W. Haddon and W. G. T. Shedd, in *Basic Writings of Saint Augustine*, vol. 2, ed. W. J. Oates (New York: Random House, 1948).

4. Ibid., VII.6.

5. Ibid., XV.8–9, 21.

6. Ibid., XV.21.

7. Ibid., XV.9.

8. Ibid., XV.11.

9. Ibid., VIII.10.

10. Ibid., IX.3.

11. Ibid., X.11–12.

12. Ibid., XIV.2, 10.

13. Cf. ibid., XIV.18, 12; XII.6; XII.5.

14. Ibid., XV.18. Regarding this "inborn affinity," see Plato, *The Seventh Letter*, from which Augustine was likely quoting.

15. Augustine, *De Trinitate*, VIII.10; cf. VIII.7–9; X.2f; IX.2f, 4.

16. Other examples can be found in Jung, "Answer to Job," *CW*, XI, passim.

17. This is also known as the Athanasian Creed.

18. Tom F. Driver, "Spirit, God and Christ: Toward a Trinitarian Ethic," *Christ in a Changing World: Toward an Ethical Christology* (New York: Crossroad, 1981), 102f.

19. Wallace Stevens, "Thirteen Ways of Looking at a Blackbird," *Collected Poems* (New York: Alfred A. Knopf, 1975), 93.

20. Novalis, "When Numbers, Figures, No More Hold the Key," in *An Anthology of German Poetry from Hölderlin to Rilke*, ed. Angel Fiores (Garden City: Doubleday, 1960), 55.

21. Augustine, *De Trinitate*, XV.20.

22. Ibid., XV.11.

23. Ibid., IX.1.

24. Ibid., XV.23.

25. Ibid. Cf. ibid., XII.5, 12, where Augustine says that the Trinity is not actual marriage but "the hidden wedlock" of man and woman within each self.

26. Martin Heidegger, *Identity and Difference*, trans. J. Stambaugh (New York: Harper & Row, 1969), 21. (The German is on p. 84 of the same edition.)

27. Ibid., 29 (German, 92).

28. Ibid.

29. Ibid., 32 (German, 104).

30. Ibid., 37 (German, 102).

31. Beda Allemann, "Metaphor and Antimetaphor," in *Interpretation: The Poetry of Meaning*, ed. S. R. Hopper and D. L. Miller (New York: Harcourt, Brace, and World, 1967), 103–24.

32. Stanley Romaine Hopper, "The Bucket As It Is," *Metaphor and Beyond* (Syracuse: Syracuse University Department of Religion, 1979), 5–48. Philip Wheelright, *Metaphor and Reality* (Bloomington: Indiana University Press, 1962), 78–86, and passim.

33. Jacques Derrida, *Of Grammatology*, trans. G. C. Spivak (Baltimore: Johns Hopkins University Press, 1976), passim.

34. Harold Bloom, "The Breaking of Form," *Deconstruction and Criticism* (New York: Continuum, 1979), 1–38.

35. Julián Marías, "Philosophic Truth and the Metaphoric System," in *Interpretation*, 46f.

36. Jung, *CW*, VII. Compare paragraph 476 with paragraph 260.

37. Ibid., VII.224. Cf. 111f, 240, 389, 454, 464.

38. Ibid., VII.112.

39. Ibid.

40. Ibid., VII.269. Cf. Jung, "Commentary on Kundalini Yoga," *Spring 1975*, 31: "Individuation is not that you become an ego; you would then be an individualist. An individualist is a man who did not succeed in individuating; he is a philosophically distilled egotist, whilst individuation is becoming that thing which is not the ego, and that is very strange. Nobody understands what the Self is, because the Self is just what you are not — it is not the ego. . . . If you function through your Self you are not yourself — that is what you feel. You have to do it as if you were a stranger."

41. Plotinus, *Enneads*, I.ii.2, trans. A. H. Armstrong (Cambridge: Harvard University Press, 1978).

42. Ibid., I.ii.6f.

43. See Plotinus, *Enneads*, II.v.3; V.viii.9, 13; VI.ix.9.

44. Augustine, *On Free Will*, XXI.60, trans. J. H. S. Burleigh (Philadelphia: Westminster Press, 1953).

45. Augustine, *De Trinitate*, XII.5.12.

46. James Hillman, "An Essay on Pan," *Pan and the Nightmare* (Dallas: Spring Publications, 1972), xxxix. Cf. Freud's proposal to "equate phantasy and reality," pt. 1, interlude, n. 8.

47. Nicholas Berdyaev, *The Divine and the Human* (London: Geoffrey Bles, 1969), 44.

### 3

### THE TRAGIC
### VISION OF THE TRINITY

1. This idea is amplified in D. L. Miller, *The New Polytheism* (Dallas: Spring Publications, 1981); cf. Miller, "Theology's Ego/Religion's Soul," *Spring 1980*, 78–89.

2. See Jung, *CW*, XIII.270. This is actually from a late source and may refer to a mortal hero rather than to the god Hermes. An epigram from the Roman rhetorician Martial (Book V.24) reads, *"Hermes omnia solus et ter unus."* This seems to refer to a gladiator rather than to a deity.

3. Erich Neumann, *Origins and History of Consciousness*, trans. R. F. C. Hull, vol. 1 (New York: Harper & Row, 1962), 216 n. 22. This is also likened to the Egyptian trinity of Osiris, Isis, and Set.

4. *The Orphic Hymns*, XV (XIV): "All things round thy head exalted shine. / The earth is thine and . . . / The sea profound" (trans. Thomas

Taylor). New archaeological evidence from a pyre in Thessalonike places this mythologem much earlier than heretofore believed. The Derveni Papyrus dates from the fourth century but may be as early as the sixth. See *REG*, LXXXVII (1974), 91–110; *Deltion*, XIX (1964), 17–25. Scholars have assumed that this was a Christian trinitarian influence on late Hellenistic Orphism, but it may be that the Old Neoplatonists were closer to the truth in their belief that Orphism influenced Christian doctrine.

5. *Homeric Hymns* (Dionysos III), trans. C. Boer (Dallas: Spring Publications, 1979), 17.

6. Hesiod, *Theogony*, trans. N. O. Brown (Bloomington: Library of Liberal Arts, 1953), passim.

7. James Ogilvy, *Many-Dimensional Man* (New York: Oxford University Press, 1977), 141.

8. Norman O. Brown, "Trinity," chap. 3 in *Love's Body* (New York: Random House, 1966).

9. Carl Kerényi, "Die Göttin Natur," *Eranos 14–1946*.

10. It is especially noteworthy that this term "round dance" *(perichorēsis)* is precisely the term used by the church fathers to speak of the relationship between the "persons" of the Trinity. See, for example, Augustine, *De Trinitate*, IX.5.

11. Carl Kerényi, *Goddesses of Sun and Moon*, trans. M. Stein (Dallas: Spring Publications, 1979), 77.

12. See Carl Kerényi, *Zeus and Hera: Archetypal Image of Father, Husband, Wife*, trans. C. Holme (Princeton: Princeton University Press, 1975), 50–58; and *The Gods of the Greeks* (London: Thames and Hudson, 1979), 11.

13. See Jung, *CW*, XI.177f; Helmuth Jacobsohn, "Das Gespräch eines Lebensmüden mit seinem Ba," *Zeitlose Dokumente der Seele* (Zurich: C. G. Jung-Institut, 1952), and "Die dogmatische Stellung des Königs in der Theologie der alten Ägypter," *Aegyptische Forschungen*, ed. A. Scharff (Hamburg: Gluckstadt, Heft 8, 1939); Friedrich Preisigke, *Vom Göttlichen Fluidum nach Ägyptischer Anschauung* (Berlin: Papyrusinstitut Heidelberg, Schrift I, 1920).

14. Xenophanes, frag. 11 (Sextus, *Adv. math.*, IX.193). Aristophanes, *Clouds*, 1079–1081. Cf. Clement of Alexandria, *Protrepticus*, passim.

15. A similar view has been argued by James Hillman in "Schism." See also part 1, interlude, n. 41 in this book.

16. Mark 15:34; Matt. 27:46. Cf. Ps. 22:1.

17. John 16:7.

18. Arthur C. McGill, *Suffering: A Test of Theological Method* (Philadelphia: Westminster Press, 1982), 66.

19. Ibid., 74.

20. Ibid., 77.

21. Ibid., 78.

22. Ibid.

23. Rainer Maria Rilke, *Sonnets to Orpheus*, 1.7, my trans.

24. James Hillman, *The Myth of Analysis* (Evanston: Northwestern University Press, 1972), 196; cf. Miller, "Theology's Ego/Religion's Soul."

25. Jung, *CW*, XIV.778.

26. Throughout this section I am deeply indebted to the assistance of two colleagues at Syracuse University: Patricia Cox, for her researches and insights in a seminar that we taught together on the subject of the Trinity (1979); and Stephen Simmer, for his dissertation, *Hekate and Scholarship: Towards an Imaginal Sociology of Education* (Syracuse University, 1980). See "The Academy of the Dead," *Spring 1981*, 89–106. Also see J. Heckenbach, "Hekate," *Pauly's Real-Encyclopädie der klassischen Altertumswissenschaften*, ed. G. Wissowa and W. Kroll; and H. Steundig, "Hekate," *Ausführliches Lexikon der Griechischen und Römischen Mythologie*, vol. 1, pt. 2. For the material on *achos*, see Simmer, *Hekate*, 63.

27. Simmer, *Hekate*, 60ff.

28. *The Orphic Hymns* (Hekate), I.1–2.

29. Hesiod, *Theogony*, 411ff.

30. Nichomachus of Gerasa, *Introduction to Arithmetic*, trans. M. L. D'Ooge (Ann Arbor: University of Michigan Press, 1938), 103, 105. For another exposition of the "between," see D. L. Miller, "Rhythms of Silenos in a Poetics of Christ," *Eranos 47–1978*.

31. See Strabo, *Geog.*, 468; Cf. Steundig, "Hekate," 1886; Simmer, *Hekate*, 56f.

32. Carl Kerényi, *Hermes: Guide of Souls*, trans. M. Stein (Zurich: Spring Publications, 1976), 65.

33. *Homeric Hymns* (Demeter), 16f. Cf. Lucian, *Philops.*, 24; *Schol. Theocrit.*, II.12; Virgil, *Aeneid*, VI.118, 564; Simmer, *Hekate*, passim; C. Kerényi, "Kore," in Jung and Kerényi, *Essays on a Science of Mythology*, trans. R. F. C. Hull (New York: Harper & Row, 1963), 113; M. P. Nilsson, *Greek Folk Religion* (New York: Harper & Row, 1961), 111; Erwin Rhode, *Psyche*, trans. W. B. Hillis (New York: Harper & Row, 1966), vol. 2, app. 6, 590ff.

34. This has been deduced from Sophocles, *Antigone*, 1199.

35. *Homeric Hymns* (Demeter), 58; *Schol. Theocrit.*, II.12; Chrysostom, *Orat.*, IV.90; Rhode, *Psyche*; Steundig, "Hekate," 1893f. Cf. Simmer, *Hekate*, 62.

36. See Heckenbach, "Hekate," 2775; cf. Simmer, *Hekate*, 127f.

37. Cf. James Hillman, "Dream and the Underworld," *Eranos 42–1973*, and *The Dream and the Underworld* (New York: Harper & Row, 1979), 23–67.

INTERLUDE

LIMINALITY, BOUNDARY,
AND THE BETWEEN

1. Henry Corbin, "The *Imago Templi* and Secular Norms," trans. R. Horine, *Spring 1975*, 175.

2. Arthur Koestler, *The Act of Creation* (New York: Macmillan, 1964), 124ff.

3. Cited in Arthur Koestler, 125, from *Mysterium cosmographicum*, preface, 4.

4. Ibid.

5. Ibid.

6. Cited in Koestler, 126, from *Opera omnia*, XIII, 33f.

7. Koestler, 127. It is interesting in this regard to note that Newton, "standing on the shoulders of giants" (*i.e.*, Kepler), studied theology seriously at Cambridge in the 1670s, and embarked on a program of diatribe against "the false doctrine of the Trinity" in the name of the true meaning of the Bible, namely, apocalypse! This story has been admirably chronicled by Richard S. Westfall in "Newton's Marvelous Years of Discovery and their Aftermath: Myth versus Manuscript," *Isis* 71, 256 (March 1980): 109–21. "Single vision and Newton's sleep"(!).

8. Gaston Bachelard, *The Philosophy of No: A Philosophy of the New Scientific Mind*, trans. G. C. Waterston (New York: Orion, 1968), 104, 106.

9. Ibid., 107.

10. Ibid., 108.

11. Ibid., 109.

12. Ibid., 110.

13. Gary Zukav, *The Dancing Wu Li Masters: An Overview of the New Physics* (New York: William Morrow, 1979), 89.

14. Werner Heisenberg, *Physics and Philosophy* (New York: Harper & Row, 1958), 41. See Zukav, *Dancing Wu Li Masters*, 90; cf. 273, 285.

15. Zukav, *Dancing Wu Li Masters*, 257.

16. Ibid., 103.

17. John Von Neumann, *The Mathematical Foundations of Quantum Mechanics*, trans. R. Beyer (Princeton: Princeton University Press, 1955), 253. See Zukav, *Dancing Wu Li Masters*, 274.

18. From Esalen tapes, Conference on Physics and Consciousness, Big Sur, Calif., Jan. 1976, in Zukav, *Dancing Wu Li Masters*, 284.

19. Ibid., 286.

20. Ibid., 89.

21. Cited in Heisenberg, *Physics and Philosophy*, 206. See Zukav, *Dancing Wu Li Masters*, 275.

22. See, for example, Karl Jaspers, "Limit Situations" (from *Psychologie der Weltanschauungen*) in *The Worlds of Existentialism*, ed. M. Friedman (New York: Random House, 1964), 100ff; Martin Heidegger, "The Limitation of Being," *An Introduction to Metaphysics*, trans. R. Manheim (Garden City: Doubleday, 1961), 79ff; Paul Tillich, *What is Religion?* (New York: Harper & Row, 1969), 150: "Neither formlessness nor domination by an alien form . . . the import of the Unconditional is to break forth and shatter form, not formlessly but paradoxically. Life within this highest of tensions is life from God. Intuition of this infinite paradox is thinking about God." Cf. the

# NOTES 147

section on "the boundary situation" in *The Protestant Era*, trans. J. L. Adams (Chicago: University of Chicago Press, 1957), 195ff.

23. Charles E. Scott, *Boundaries in Mind: A Study of Immediate Awareness Based on Psychotherapy* (New York: Crossroad, 1982), esp. chap. 3, "Accord and Discord on the Border."

24. Charles E. Winquist, "Body, Text, and Imagination," *Deconstruction and Theology*, ed. T. J. J. Altizer et al. (New York: Crossroad, 1982), esp. 51–56.

25. The reference is to Kaufman's work, *An Essay on Theological Method* (Missoula: Scholars Press, 1979), x. Cf. the treatment of the Trinity in its function vis à vis the rapprochement of science and religion in James W. Jones, *The Redemption of Matter* (Lanham, Md.: University Press of America, 1984), 28–32.

26. Gordon Kaufman, "Transcendence Without Mythology," *Harvard Theological Review* 59 (1966): 105–32; and *God the Problem* (Cambridge; Harvard University Press, 1972), chap. 3.

27. Kaufman, *God the Problem*, 47, 49.

28. Ibid., 61.

29. Ibid., 70 n. 30.

30. Paul M. Van Buren, *Theological Explorations* (New York: Macmillan, 1968), 161ff.

31. Ibid., 166, 168, 169, 170.

32. Ibid., 178–80.

33. Paul M. Van Buren, *The Edges of Language* (New York: Macmillan, 1972).

34. Ibid., 82.

35. Cf. C. S. Lewis, "At the Fringe of Language," *Studies in Words* (New York: Cambridge University Press, 1960), 214ff.

36. W. H. Auden, *Homage to Clio* (New York: Random House, 1960), 50f.

37. John Wisdom, *Philosophy and Psychoanalysis* (Oxford: Basil Blackwell, 1953), 282.

38. Van Buren, *The Edges of Language*, 110; cf. n. 31 above.

39. Ibid., 147.

40. Ibid., 144.

41. T. S. Eliot, "East Coker," *Four Quartets* (New York: Harcourt Brace, 1943).

42. Arnold van Gennep, *The Rites of Passage*, trans M. B. Vizedom and G. L. Caffee (London: Routledge and Kegan Paul, 1960); cf. Victor Turner, *The Ritual Process, Structure and Anti-Structure* (Chicago: Aldine Publishing, 1969), esp. chap. 3, "Liminality and Communitas."

43. Turner, *The Ritual Process*, 95, 97, 106.

44. Martin Buber, *Between Man and Man*, trans. R. G. Smith (New York: Macmillan, 1965), 204; cf. 98, 203f; and Turner, *The Ritual Process*, 127.

45. Turner, *The Ritual Process*, 95, 125. Cf. Turner, "Betwixt and Between: The Liminal Period in *Rites de Passage*," *The Forest of Symbols*

(Ithaca: Cornell University Press, 1975), 93–111; also, *Revelation and Divination in Ndembu Ritual* (Ithaca: Cornell University Press, 1975), 33, 189.

46. Turner, *The Ritual Process*, 107f; cf. 145f.

47. Turner, *Revelation and Divination*, 33.

48. Wendy Doniger O'Flaherty, "Inside and Outside the Mouth of God: The Boundary between Myth and Reality," *Daedalus* (Spring 1980): 101, 102, 111. Cf. Gaston Bachelard, "The Dialectics of Inside and Outside," *The Poetics of Space*, trans. M. Jolas (New York: Orion Press, 1964), 211–31; Rudolf Arnheim and Wolfgang Zucker, "Inside and Outside in Architecture: A Symposium," *Journal of Aesthetics and Art Criticism* 25, 1 (Fall 1966): 3–15.

49. O'Flaherty, "Inside and Outside," 98.

50. *Bhagavada Purana* 10.8.21–45. Cited in O'Flaherty, "Inside and Outside," 95. Cf. O'Flaherty, *Hindu Myths* (Hammondsworth: Penguin Books, 1975); and *Women, Androgynes, and Other Mythical Beasts* (Chicago: University of Chicago Press, 1980). Compare similar episodes of discovering a world inside the mouth in Lucian, *True History*, I.30ff; and Rabelais, *Gargantua and Pantagruel*, chap. 32. For an exposition of this theme, see Erich Auerbach, *Mimesis*, trans. W. Trask (Garden City: Doubleday, 1953), chap. 11.

51. O'Flaherty, "Inside and Outside," 96.

52. Cited in Jonathan Z. Smith, "I Am A Parrot (Red)," *History of Religions* 11.4 (May 1972): 406.

53. Claude Lévi-Strauss, "The Structural Study of Myth," *Structural Anthropology*, trans. C. Jacobson and B. G. Schoepf (Garden City: Doubleday, 1967), 220f.

54. Ibid., 226f. The trinitarian model has drawn theoretical attention not only in the field of anthropology but also in sociology. Most remarkable in this regard is the work by Max Stackhouse in utilizing the paradigm of the Trinity for a reconstruction of "urban ethos." Stackhouse writes that the *credo* presents a pertinent option to the city, "an option now nearly lost in the divorce of theology from the foundations of social theory, but one which can be recovered by reconstruction of the doctrine of the Trinity." The Trinity succeeds where other socio-ethical models fail, he notes, because "the ultimate meta-ethical model must be pluralistic, but it must have a coherence that does not allow the parts to fly into fragmented pluralism. . . . This use [by sociologists and ethicists] of the model of the Trinity permits the fundamental possibility of diversity within unity and unity within diversity that urban ethos cries for." Stackhouse concludes with a lament and a hope: "The modern city is not these things. The secular city is not and perhaps never shall be all of these; but in the midst of the terribly mundane, anonymous, pragmatic features of urban life, there are embedded the tracks of the Divine [what this work calls *vestigia trinitatis*], and the decisive patterns of experience that reveal a sacred 'rightness' about the city. These patterns are capable of being identified through a reconstructed *credo*" (Max Stackhouse, *Ethics and the Urban Ethos* [Boston: Beacon Press, 1972], 119, 132, 140f).

55. J. Hillis Miller, "The Critic as Host," *Deconstruction and Criticism,*
ed. G. Hartman (New York: Seabury, 1979), 217–54, esp. 231, 243, 245.

56. Ibid., 231.

57. Ibid. Miller explains: "Deconstruction does not provide an escape
from nihilism, nor from metaphysics, nor from their uncanny inherence in
one another. There is no escape. It does, however, move back and forth
within this inherence. It makes the inherence oscillate in such a way that one
enters a strange borderland, a frontier region which seems to give the widest
glimpse into the other land ('beyond metaphysics'), though this land may not
by any means be entered and does not exist for Western man. . . . It is as
if the 'prisonhouse of language' were like that universe finite but unbounded
which some modern cosmologies posit. One may move everywhere freely
within this enclosure without ever encountering a wall, and yet it is limited.
It is a prison, a milieu without origin or edge. Such a place is therefore all
frontier zone without either peaceful homeland, in one direction, land of
hosts and domesticity, nor, in the other direction, any alien land of hostile
strangers, 'beyond the line.' The place we inhabit, wherever we are, is always
this in-between zone, place of host and parasite, neither inside nor outside.
It is a region of the *Unheimlich,* beyond any formalism, which reforms itself
wherever we are, if we know where we are. This 'place' is where we are, in
whatever text, in the most inclusive sense of that word, we happen to be
living. This may be made to appear, however, only by an extreme interpretation of that text. . . . (ibid.). Between metaphysics and nihilism, deconstructionist interpretation may be seen as "a new threefold way." Miller is reticent
at this point (p. 230), though Bachelard has made the matter compelling in
his *Philosophy of No,* chapters 5 and 6.

58. Harold Bloom, "The Breaking of Form," *Deconstruction and Criticism,* 1–38, esp. 1–2, 14.

59. John Ashbery, "Self-Portrait in a Convex Mirror," cited in ibid., 30. On
this theme of vanishing, see D. L. Miller, "Theologia Imaginalis," *The
Archeology of the Imagination: Deconstruction and Hermeneutics,* ed. C.
Winquist (Chico: Scholars Press, 1981).

60. James Hillman, "Further Notes on Images," *Spring 1978,* 181f.
Hillman has borrowed this idea of the "hiatus" from an observation by
Robert Grinnell on one of Jung's dreams. See Grinnell, "Reflections on the
Archetype of Consciousness," *Spring 1970,* 19.

61. Rainer Maria Rilke, *Sonnets to Orpheus,* II.12. Cf. Miller, "Theologia
Imaginalis," passim.

62. Justus George Lawler, *Celestial Pantomime: Poetic Structures of Transcendence* (New Haven: Yale University Press, 1979), 46.

63. Ibid., 59f.

64. Ibid., 92.

65. William V. Spanos, "The Detective and the Boundary; Some Notes on
the Postmodern Literary Imagination," *boundary 2* 1, 1 (Fall 1972): 147–68.

66. Ibid., 150.

67. Ibid. Note also the criticism by Spanos of "narrative form," and com-

pare Ted L. Estess, "The Inenarrable Contraption: Reflections on the Metaphor of Story," *Journal of the American Academy of Religion* 42, 3 (September 1974): 415–34; Patricia Berry, "An Approach to the Dream," *Spring 1974*, 68–71; and D. L. Miller, "Introduction to the Second Edition," *The New Polytheism* (Dallas: Spring Publications, 1981).

68. Spanos contrasts modernism with postmodernism by likening the former to "fear" which knows its object and the latter to "dread," where it is "nothing" (no-thing) that is feared. The second of these is, therefore, more thoroughgoing and radical. See Spanos, "The Detective and the Boundary," 148ff.

69. Ibid., 158.

70. Ibid., 148, 154, 156, 158, 166, 167f. But for a different view of the archetypal image of the detective, see Amy Brill, *Remembering Mysteries: The Nineteenth-Century Detective Story as a Modern Art of Memory* (Ph.D. diss., Syracuse: Syracuse University, 1978).

71. In spite of his orientation in the direction of historical culture-criticism, Spanos also opens the way to his perspective when he lists works by Euripides, Wycherley, Dickens, Tolstoy, Dostoevski, Pirandello, and Eliot as former instances of postmodernism (Spanos, "The Detective and the Boundary," 151).

72. Stanley R. Hopper, "Symbolic Reality and the Poet's Task," *Eranos 34–1965*, 108–218.

73. Ibid., 181.

74. Ludwig Wittgenstein, *Philosophical Investigations* (Oxford: Basil Blackwell, 1958), pt. 1, 48, 48e; cf. Hopper, "Symbolic Reality," 185.

75. Hopper, "Symbolic Reality," 211. Cf. D. L. Miller, "Hades and Dionysos: The Poetry of Soul," *Journal of the American Academy of Religion* 46, 3 (September 1978): 331–35, in which there is meditated the saying of Emerson, "the poet turns the world to glass."

76. Cf. James Hillman, "Psychologizing or Seeing Through," pt. 3 in *Re-Visioning Psychology* (New York: Harper & Row, 1975).

77. Stanley R. Hopper, "Jerusalem's Wall and Other Perimeters," *Humanities, Religion, and the Arts Tomorrow*, ed. H. Hunter (New York: Holt Rinehart & Winston, 1972), 228–45.

78. The lines are from William Blake's poem, "Jerusalem," cited in Hopper, "Jerusalem's Wall," 229.

79. Hopper, "Jerusalem's Wall," 231.

80. Stanley R. Hopper, "The Bucket As It Is," *Metaphor and Beyond* (Syracuse: Syracuse University Department of Religion, 1979), esp. 40, 43ff.

4

ANGEL FACE AND BODY

1. Plato, *The Republic* IX (588D); cf. E. R. Dodds, "*The Parmenides* of Plato and the Origin of the Neoplatonic One," *Classical Quarterly* 22

(July–October 1928), 129ff.

2. Plato, *Philebus*, 26C–D, trans. R. Hackworth, in *The Collected Dialogues of Plato*, ed. E. Hamilton and H. Cairns (Princeton: Princeton University Press, 1961).

3. Plato, *Timaeus*, 31B–C.

4. Ibid., 34B.

5. Plotinus, *Enneads*, V.iii.5, trans. S. MacKenna (London: Faber & Faber, 1971).

6. Ibid., V.viii.9.

7. Plotinus, *Enneads*, III.ix.1, trans. A. H. Armstrong (Cambridge: Harvard University Press, 1967).

8. Plotinus, *Enneads*, V.viii.13, trans. MacKenna; cf. VI.ix.9. See R. T. Wallis, *Neoplatonism* (London: Duckworth, 1972), on Plotinus and the Trinity (57–60, 110ff), and on the Neoplatonic triads of spirit/soul/body, one/intellect/soul, emanation/logos/sympathy, substance/potentiality/actuality, and abiding/procession/revision (pp. 72, 95, 106, 123, 130–34, 154, 171). The last of these triads (*monē/proodos/epistrophē*) has been further explicated, and importantly so, by Proclus. See *Elements of Theology*, prop. 35 and passim. See also J. Patrick Atherton, "The Neoplatonic 'One' and the Trinitarian 'Arche,' " and A. H. Armstrong, "The Apprehension of Divinity in the Self and Cosmos in Plotinus," *The Significance of Neoplatonism*, ed. R. B. Harris (Norfolk: International Society for Neoplatonic Studies, 1976), 173–98.

9. Proclus, *Elements of Theology*, prop. 148, trans. E. R. Dodds, (Oxford: At the Clarendon Press, 1963).

10. Proclus, *The Elements of Theology*, commentary on prop. 20, 206ff, and prop. 35, 220ff.

11. D. P. Walker, *The Ancient Theology* (Ithaca: Cornell University Press, 1972).

12. Ibid., 6, 14, passim.

13. Also note the saying of Plato in the *Republic:* "Join the three in one" (IX.588D).

14. Pseudo-Dionysius, *Div. nom.*, IV.14.

15. Erigena, *De div. nat.*, 152A.

16. Psellus, *CMAG*, VI.165.36ff.

17. See Frances Yates, "The Art of Ramon Lull," *Journal of the Warburg and Courtauld Institutes* 17 (1954): 115–73; *The Art of Memory* (Chicago: University of Chicago Press, 1966), 173–98.

18. See Walker, *The Ancient Theology;* and Frances Yates, *The Occult Philosophy in the Elizabethan Age* (London: Routledge and Kegan Paul, 1979), passim.

19. Yates, *Occult Philosophy*, passim.

20. Ibid., and Richard S. Westfall, "Newton's Marvellous Years of Discovery and Their Aftermath: Myth versus Manuscript," *Isis* 76, 256 (March 1980): 109ff. Cf. Titus Burckhardt's explication of Trinity in the work of the

mystic Ruysbroek, *On the Adornment of the Spiritual Marriage*, in *Alchemy: Science of the Cosmos, Science of the Soul* (Baltimore: Penguin Books, 1974), 71f.

21. See Yates, *Occult Philosophy*, 95ff.

22. Pierre Hadot, "Être, Vie, Pensée chez Plotin et avant Plotin," *Les Sources de Plotin* (Entretiens V, Foundation Hardt, Vandoeuvres-Genève, 1960), 127 and passim; and "Comm. on Marius Victorinus," *Traités theologiques sur la Trinité*, 2 vols., (Paris, 1960); Ewert Cousins, "The Trinity and Creation," *Bonaventure and the Coincidence of Opposites* (Chicago: Franciscan Herald Press, 1978), 97–130, esp. 101; John D. Turner, "The Gnostic Threefold Path to Enlightenment," *Novum Testamentum* 22 (1980), 324–51; Peter Manchester, "The Noetic Triad in Plotinus, Marius Victorinus, and Augustine"; and John D. Turner, "Gnosticism and Platonism: The Platonizing Sethian Texts from Nag Hammadi in Their Relation to Later Platonic Literature." These last two essays are presentations made to the International Conference on Neoplatonism and Gnosticism, March 18–21, 1984, in Norman, Oklahoma, forthcoming in a volume to be titled, *Neoplatonism and Gnosticism*, published under the auspices of the International Society for Neoplatonic Studies. (N. 8 in Manchester's text recommends a work on the same topic by Jay Bregman, "Trinity versus Quaternity in Later Neoplatonism," a presentation to the working group on Platonism and Neoplatonism of the American Academy of Religion at the annual meeting, December 22, 1983.)

23. See *The Nag Hammadi Library*, ed. J. Robinson (New York: Harper & Row, 1977).

24. See John Dillon, "Origen's Doctrine of the Trinity and Some Later Neoplatonic Theories," *Neoplatonism and Christian Thought*, ed. D. O'Meara (Norfolk: International Society of Neoplatonic Studies, 1982), 19–23.

25. Cf. Proclus, *Elements of Theology*, prop. 117: "Every God is a measure of existing things."

26. "Commentary on Plato's Symposium," first speech, chap. 1, trans. S. Jayne (University of Missouri Studies, XIX, 1, 1944), 133. Ficino in this regard, like so many others, cites Virgil: "God rejoices in odd numbers" (*Eclogues*, VIII.76).

27. Cited in Walker, *The Ancient Theology*, 110.

28. See Walker, *The Ancient Theology*, 37 and passim; and Yates, *Occult Philosophy*, 32, 33, 36, 65, 100, and passim.

29. Jean Daniélou, "Trinité et angélologie dans la théologie judéo-chrétienne," *Recherches des sciences religieuses* 45 (1957): 5ff. Cf. J. Barbel, *Christos angelos* (Bonn: P. Hanstein, 1941). It should be noted that Daniélou's perspective on this material is opposite to the Neoplatonic one. He is concerned with linking Christian doctrine to Jewish backgrounds (in this case, the angelology of the later prophets Zechariah, Daniel, and Ezekiel), hence with purging the doctrine of Neoplatonic paganism. But, see Henry Corbin on the Ebionite tradition of *Christos angelos* for a Neoplatonic read-

ing of this same material in "Nécessité de l'angélologie," *L'Ange et l'homme* (Paris: Albin Michel, 1978), 31–53.

30. See J. N. Kelly, *Early Christian Doctrines* (New York: Harper & Row, 1978), 256f.

31. For the sources of this Eastern iconographic tradition, see Alan Watts, *Myth and Ritual in Christianity* (New York: Grove Press, 1960), 31 n. 3; and *Russian Icons: The Collection of George R. Hahn* (Pittsburgh: Carnegie Institute Press, 1944), item 28 and passim.

32. Cf. Paul Tillich, *Systematic Theology*, vol. 1. (Chicago: University of Chicago Press, 1951), 229; and Corbin, "Nécessité de l'angélologie."

33. Cf. the important articulation of this perspective in Curtis Bennett, *God as Form: Essays in Greek Theology* (Albany: State University of New York Press, 1976).

34. Cf. Henry Corbin, *Creative Imagination in the Sufism of Ibn 'Arabi*, trans. R. Manheim (Princeton: Princeton University Press, 1969), 292 n. 10.

35. Bennett, *God as Form*, 217. "Those shapes are individual, if emerging from contemporary forms of discourse, and both go back, at last, to the great Gods and Goddesses, the enduring forms for human recognition of each and every sort of pressure" (ibid.).

36. Corbin, "Nécessité de l'angélologie," 66. Cf. James Hillman, "Egalitarian Typologies versus the Perception of the Unique," *Eranos 45–1976*, 246ff.

37. Corbin, "Nécessité de l'angélologie," 68.

38. C. S. Lewis, *Till We Have Faces: A Myth Retold* (Grand Rapids: Eerdmans, 1956), 294.

39. For a documentation of this identification of angel and image, see D. L. Miller, "Theologia Imaginalis," *The Archeology of the Imagination: Deconstruction and Hermeneutics*, ed. C. Winquist (Chico: Scholars Press, 1981). On the notion of angel in relation to imagination, see two works by Roberts Avens, "Things and Angels: Death and Immortality in Heidegger and in Islamic Gnosis," *Hamdard Islamicus* VII.2 (1984): 3–32; and *The New Gnosis: Heidegger, Hillman, and Angels* (Dallas: Spring Publications, 1984).

40. John 10:7.

41. See chap. 1, n. 22.

42. See Wallis, *Neoplatonism*, 5f, 61, 63.

43. Ps. 69:1–2.

44. M. Berthelot, ed., *Collection des anciens alchimistes grec* (Osnabruck: Zeller, 1967), 230.

45. Plato, *Timaeus*, 31B–32C.

46. *Turba philosophorum*, trans. A. E. Waite (London: Rider, 1914), 25.

47. Hajime Nakamura, *Parallel Developments: A Comparative History of Ideas* (Tokyo: Kodansha, 1975), 59.

48. Mircea Eliade, *Gods, Goddesses, and Myths of Creation* (New York: Harper & Row, 1974), 88ff, passim.

49. Patricia Berry, "An Approach to the Dream," *Echo's Subtle Body: Contributions to Archetypal Psychology* (Dallas: Spring Publications, 1982), 59, 70.

50. James Hillman, *The Dream and the Underworld* (New York: Harper & Row, 1979), 134.

51. James Hillman, "Psychotherapy's Inferiority Complex," *Eranos 46–1977*, 166; cf. *The Dream and the Underworld*, 169: "The process of releasing soul from literal interiority goes hand in hand with coagulating it."

52. Edward Edinger, "Psychotherapy and Alchemy, IV: Coagulatio," *Quadrant* (Summer 1979).

53. Jung, *Letters*, vol. 1, 65f.

54. Ibid., vol. 2, 557.

55. Martin Ruland, *A Lexicon of Alchemy*, trans. A. E. Waite (London: Watkins, 1964), 107. Cf. Alison Coudert, *Alchemy: The Philosopher's Stone* (Boulder: Shambala, 1980), 88, for alchemical references to trinity.

56. Nichomachus of Gerasa, *Introduction to Arithmetic*, trans. M. L. D'Ooge (Ann Arbor: University of Michigan Press, 1938), 261–62 n. 6.

57. *The Compact Edition of the Oxford English Dictionary*, vol. 1 (New York: Oxford, 1971), 447.

58. Ibid., from John Donne, *Pseudo-martyrdom*.

59. Ibid., vol. 2, 2490.

60. Edward Edinger, "Psychotherapy and Alchemy," 29. I am indebted in the extreme to Edinger's researches for many of the references in this section of the book, although the perspective here differs from Edinger's in two important respects. First, coagulation here is not identified solely with ego development as it seems to be in Edinger's work. Second, where Edinger identifies the process of *coagulatio* with the element earth, the present perspective would see each and every element as needing coagulation—just as there is an earthy person who lacks body, being superficially crass or literal, so there could be fiery or watery or airy individuals whose fire, moisture, and spirit have no body to them. Theologically speaking, the difference between the present perspective and that of Edinger has to do with a differentiating of *coagulatio* in theological alchemy and incarnationalism in orthodox theology. Incarnationalist perspectives in religion, particularly in the Christian religion, may lead to historical literalism (literalizing of body historicistically and fundamentalistically), whereas the analogical and imaginal ways in alchemy could only view body as a metaphor of soul. In fact, the alchemical and Neoplatonic perspective in theology will always resist every fundamentalism, literalism, historicism, and incarnationalism—whether in theology or in psychology.

61. Jung, *CW*, XIV.321–23; cf. V.198 and IV.106.

5

TIGERS AND GHOSTS

1. Justus George Lawler, *Celestial Pantomime: Poetic Structures of Transcendence* (New Haven: Yale University Press, 1979), 92.

2. See Ernst Curtius, *European Literature and the Latin Middle Ages*, trans. W. Trask (New York: Harper & Row, 1963), 313; Maureen Quilligan,

*The Language of Allegory* (Ithaca: Cornell University Press, 1979), 160.

3. James Thurber, "*What* Cocktail Party?" *Thurber Country* (New York: Simon & Schuster, 1953), 219.

4. Ibid., 226f.

5. Wallace Stevens, "Adagia," *Opus Posthumous* (New York: Alfred A. Knopf, 1977), 173; cf. D. L. Miller, "Theologia Imaginalis," *The Archeology of the Imagination: Deconstruction and Hermeneutics*, ed. C. Winquist, (Chico: Scholars Press, 1981), 1–18.

6. This felicitous formulation is by Patricia Cox. See *Biography in Late Antiquity: The Quest for the Holy Man* (Berkeley: University of California Press, 1983), 147.

7. E. R. Wasserman, *The Finer Tone: Keats' Major Poems* (Baltimore: Johns Hopkins Press, 1953); cf. Lawler, *Celestial Pantomime*, 60.

8. Elizabeth Bieman, "Triads and Trinity in the Poetry of Robert Browning," *Neoplatonism and Christian Thought*, ed. D. J. O'Meara (Norfolk: International Society for Neoplatonic Studies, 1982).

9. Ibid.

10. José Ortega y Gassett, *Meditations on Quixote* (New York: W. W. Norton, 1961), 68f.

11. D. H. Lawrence, "Fantasia of the Unconscious," *Psychoanalysis and the Unconscious* (New York: Viking Press, 1960), 165.

12. Ibid.

13. Ibid., 202.

14. Ibid., 166.

15. Robert Creeley, "The Three Ladies," *For Love* (New York: Charles Scribners Sons, 1962), 61.

16. T. S. Eliot, "The Wasteland," *The Complete Poems and Plays* (New York: Harcourt, Brace, and World, 1952), 48.

17. Ibid., 53. Eliot adds that the particular form of expression in these lines was "stimulated by the account of one of the antarctic expeditions. . . . It was related that the party of explorers, at the extremity of their strength, had the constant delusion that there was *one more member* than could actually be counted" (ibid., 54). The biblical citation is from Luke 24:13–16.

18. Theodore Roethke, "The Happy Three," *The Collected Poems* (Garden City: Doubleday, 1975), 206f.

19. Jorge Luis Borges, "The Other Tiger," *Dreamtigers*, trans. M. Boyer and H. Morland (New York: E. P. Dutton, 1970), 70f.

20. Wallace Stevens, *Collected Poems*, 93.

21. Wallace Stevens, "Nomad Exquisite," *Collected Poems*, 94.

22. Georg Trakl, *Die Dichtungen* (Salzburg: Otto Muller, 1938), 124, my trans.

23. Martin Heidegger, "Language," *Poetry, Language, Thought*, trans. A. Hofstadter (New York: Harper & Row, 1971), 196. The original German version is "Die Sprache," *Unterwegs zur Sprache* (Pfullingen: Neske Verlag, 1975), 18f.

24. Cf. D. L. Miller, "Hades and Dionysos: The Poetry of Soul," *Journal*

*of the American Academy of Religion* 47 (September 1978); and "The Two Sandals of Christ: Descent into History and into Hell," *Eranos 50–1981*, 147–223, esp. 211ff.

25. Robert M. Pirsig, *Zen and the Art of Motorcycle Maintenance* (New York: Bantam Books, 1974), 213f.

26. Ibid., 233.

27. Ibid.

28. Ibid.

29. Ibid., 240.

30. Ibid., 296.

31. Ibid., 297.

32. Ibid.

33. Ibid., 406.

34. Ibid., inside the front cover.

35. Richard Ellman, *James Joyce* (New York: Oxford University Press, 1959).

36. Frank Budgen, *James Joyce and the Making of Ulysses* (Bloomington: Indiana University Press, 1960), 351 and passim.

37. Phillipe Sollers, "La Trinité de Joyce," *Tel Quel 83* (Spring 1980): 36–88.

38. James Joyce, *Ulysses* (New York: Random House, 1946), 205.

39. Ibid., 195.

40. In the small work, *Giacomo Joyce*, and in *Ulysses*, 121. A very different use of the same trinitarian theological structure can be seen in the writing of another Catholic novelist, Walker Percy, where a "third go-round" is struck between the dualistic options of belief and unbelief. See *The Second Coming* (New York: Pocket Books, 1981), 219–21, 312.

41. Wallace Stevens, *Opus Posthumous*, 174: "Poetry is the gaiety of language." Cf. Robert E. Doud, "The Trinity after Breakfast: Theology and Imagination in Wallace Stevens and Alfred North Whitehead," *Journal of the American Academy of Religion* 52, 3 (September 1984): 481–98.

42. Edmond Jabès, *The Book of Questions*, trans. R. Waldrop (Middletown, Conn.: Wesleyan University Press, 1976), 85ff.

43. Ramon Lull lived from 1232 to ca. 1316. This parable is from his work *Arbor scientiae*. It is presented here in the English text provided by Frances Yates, in "The Art of Ramon Lull," *Journal of the Warburg and Courtauld Institutes* 43 (1954): 150f.

## INTERLUDE
## PINTERESQUE LOVE

1. See the introduction, n. 23.

2. Samuel Beckett, *Play* (London: Faber & Faber, 1964). See D. L. Miller, "The Kingdom of Play: Some Old Theological Light from Recent Literature," *Union Seminary Quarterly Review* 25, 3 (Spring 1970): 347–52.

3. Samuel Beckett, *Ghost Trio,* in *Ends and Odds* (New York: Grove Press, 1976), 51–68; and *That Time,* ibid. I am indebted to Professor Frank Macomber of Syracuse University for information about Beethoven's "The Ghost Trio."

4. Cited in Arnold P. Hinchliffe, *Harold Pinter,* rev. ed. (Boston: Twayne Publishers, 1981), 59.

5. Harold Pinter, "Speech: Hamburg 1970," *Theatre Quarterly* 1, 3 (July–September 1971), 3.

6. Ibid., 4.

7. Harold Pinter, "Writing for the Theatre," *Complete Works: One* (New York: Grove Press, 1976), 10.

8. Harold Pinter, *Family Voices,* in *Plays: Four* (London: Eyre Methuen, 1976), 284.

9. Pinter, "Speech," 4.

10. Harold Pinter, "Writing for Myself," *Plays: Two* (London: Eyre Methuen, 1977), 10. Based on a conversation with Richard Findlater.

11. Interview cited in Martin Esslin, *The Theatre of the Absurd* (Garden City: Doubleday, 1961), 199.

12. Ibid.

13. Ibid.

14. Pinter, *The Room,* in *Complete Works: One,* 102–26.

15. Pinter, *The Birthday Party,* ibid., 17–97.

16. Pinter, *The Dumbwaiter,* ibid., 127–66.

17. Pinter, *A Slight Ache,* ibid., 167–200.

18. Pinter, *Night Out,* ibid., 201–48.

19. Pinter, *The Caretaker,* in *Plays: Two,* 13–88.

20. Pinter, *The Dwarfs,* ibid., 89–118.

21. Pinter, *The Collection,* ibid., 119–58.

22. Pinter, *The Lover,* ibid., 159–96.

23. Pinter, *Monologue,* in *Plays: Four,* 269–78.

24. Pinter, *Landscape,* in *Plays: Three* (London: Eyre Methuen, 1976), 173–98.

25. Pinter, *Dialogue for Three,* ibid., 239–40.

26. Pinter, *Silence,* ibid., 199–220.

27. Pinter, *Old Times,* in *Plays: Four,* 1–72.

28. Pinter, *Betrayal,* ibid., 155–268.

29. Ibid., 209f.

30. Pinter, *Family Voices,* ibid., 282–96.

31. To be sure, in some of the plays mentioned, as other characters have been slighted in our characterization of the trinitarian drama taking place in Pinter's plays. Yet, the motif of the erotic triangle and its fundamental drama is so central in Pinter's theatre as to make the present reading viable.

32. Pinter, *Old Times,* 25.

33. Pinter, *No Man's Land,* in *Plays: Four,* 137.

34. Ibid.

35. Ibid.
36. Shakespeare, *King Lear*, act 1, sc. 4, line 136.
37. Pinter, *Old Times*, 30, 31.
38. Pinter, *Monologue*, 273.
39. Ibid., 272.
40. Pinter, *The Dwarfs*, 100.
41. Cited in Hinchliff, *Harold Pinter*, 33.
42. Pinter, *The Dwarfs*, 111f.
43. Ibid., 112.
44. Ibid.
45. Ibid.
46. See Stanley R. Hopper, "Spirit," *Handbook of Christian Theology* (New York: Meridian Books, 1958), 357.
47. 1 Cor. 2:13.
48. William Baker and S. E. Tabachnick, *Harold Pinter* (New York: Barnes & Noble, 1973), 139.
49. Northrop Frye, *The Great Code: The Bible and Literature* (New York: Harcourt, Brace, Jovanovich, 1981), 55.


## 6
## THE BODY OF GOD

1. Cited in Karl Jaspers, *The Great Philosophers*, trans. R. Manheim (New York: Harcourt Brace, 1966), 120.
2. Ibid.
3. Nicholas of Cusa, *The Vision of God*, trans. E. G. Salter (New York: Ungar, 1969), 19.
4. Ibid., 56.
5. Ibid., 84.
6. Augustine, *Confessions*, XIII.11.
7. Nicholas of Cusa, *The Vision of God*, 58.
8. Ibid., 59f.
9. Ibid., 43f.
10. Rainer Maria Rilke, *Poems from the Book of Hours*, trans. B. Deutsch (Norfolk: New Directions, 1941), 3.
11. Ibid.
12. Nicholas of Cusa, *The Vision of God*, 84, 100; cf. 53, 55.
13. *The Heart of Thoreau's Journals*, ed. Odell Shepard (Boston: Houghton Mifflin, 1927), 48. I am grateful to Stanley Romaine Hopper for this quotation.

# INDEX

Acheron, 61
Achilles, 48
Adler, Alfred, 49
Aeginus, 57
Aeschylus, 101
Aesculapius, 7
Aglaia, 61
Agrippa, Henry C., 84
Albee, Edward, 115
Alkmene, 57
Allemann, Beda, 48
Anselm, 3
Aphrodite, 29, 30, 56, 57
Apollo, 7, 56, 57
Apostolos-Cappodona, Diane, 138
  n. 11
Apuleius, 30
Aquinas, Thomas, 112, 113
Ariadne, 7
Aristophanes, 57, 115, 144 n. 14
Aristotle, 8, 43, 75, 77
Armstrong, A. H., 151 n. 8
Arnheim, Rudolf, 148 n. 48
Artemis, 56, 57, 61
Ashbery, John, 75
Asopus, 57
Athanasius, 86
Athena, 56
Atherton, J. Patrick, 151 n. 8
Attis, 15
Auerbach, Erich, 148 n. 50

Augustine, 1, 2, 5, 6, 8, 10, 13,
  23, 25, 26, 31, 41, 42, 43, 44,
  46, 50, 57, 88, 95, 126, 131,
  136 n. 13, 139 n. 28
Avens, Roberts, 153 n. 39

Bacchus, 7
Bachelard, Gaston, 66, 68, 148
  n. 48
Barth, Karl, 59
Baynes, H. G., 34
Beckett, Samuel, 48, 76, 115, 116,
  125
Beethoven, Ludwig, 116
Bellerophon, 7
Bennett, Curtius, 86
Berdyaev, Nicholas, 13, 51
Berne, Eric, 31
Berry, Patricia, 89, 150 n. 67
Bessarion, Cardinal, 84
Beurrier, Paul, 84
Bieman, Elizabeth, 98
Blake, William, 78
Bloom, Harold, 48, 75, 77, 78
Boehme, Jacob, 13, 26, 41
Boethius, 126
Bohr, Niels, 67
Bonaventure, 84, 108
Borges, Jorge Luis, 96, 102, 103,
  105–9, 114
Brahma, 15